The Family Dinner Cookbook

Bringing Families Back Together

Janet Sandeen

THE FAMILY DINNER COOKBOOK

© 2013 by Janet Sandeen

All rights reserved. No part of this publication may be reproduced in any form without written permission from Book Villages, P.O. Box 64526, Colorado Springs, CO 80962. wwwbookvillages.com

BOOK VILLAGES and the BOOK VILLAGES logo are registered trademarks of Book Villages. Absence of ® in connection with marks of Book Villages or other parties does not indicate an absence of registration of those marks.

ISBN: 978-1-93851-216-2

Cover and Interior Design by Niddy Griddy Design, Inc.

Printed in the United States of America

17 16 15 14 13 / 1 2 3 4 5 6 7 8

Dedication

This book is dedicated to my family: Charlie my husband, Jacque, BJ, Kim & Shay, Jon & Rachel, Lisa & Ryan. I love you all so much and have loved our family time in everything that we have done! In tough times, love has brought us closer. Thank you all for your love and support!

I also dedicate this first cookbook to my parents, Ed & Joyce Waldrep. They were both cooks and passed on the love for cooking and family time to me and all my siblings. My mom was known for her baking; up to just weeks before she passed away, she was making special treats for those she loved. She could remember everyone's birthday and what his or her favorite thing was. She loved baking and sharing her goods!

My dad opened his first restaurant, Ed's Fish 'n' Chips, in 1984. You can still eat at Ed's today in Avondale, Arizona. He passed away at the young age of 51, but made such an impact on many people. He was always cooking for others! He was dearly loved and respected by all. His favorite pastime was fishing! After a fishing trip, we always had a big fish fry at home. The fish fries just got too big for their house! After 1984, Ed's became the meeting place for our family and friends!

Many of the recipes in this book came from my parents or were inspired by them. I want to thank others who submitted their recipes to include! It's so fun to share recipes that you know work and are easy to do!

A special thank you to Lisa Hamilton, my youngest daughter, for all your help and creativity for this cookbook and developing our website. You helped put my personality into it from the beginning. You're great!

A special thank you to my friends for your love and support for my crazy ideas! You are all wonderful!

Contents

Introduction	7
Helpful Hints	9
Appetizers & Sauces	15
Breads & Breakfasts	29
Beverages	49
Salads & Dressings	55
Soups & Stews	69
Main Dishes	77
Side Dishes	105
Desserts	123
Index	157

Introduction

Welcome to *The Family Dinner Cookbook!* I am so excited you have decided to use my cookbook for your family.

I hope you find it easy to follow and that you enjoy every meal you make. On a more personal level, my name is Janet and I love my family!

I work to preserve it as much as I can. I believe as we come back to the dinner table and eat as a family, our family connections grow stronger. In today's hectic day-to-day life, we are spending so much money and time eating out, which leads to not having that family time. We can eat healthier as well as save money by eating at home. When we're at the dinner table, our family conversations are very different than when we are out in public.

I believe we should cook with kids, and even dads, in the kitchen. Bring the kids in and give them a job; this will give them ownership in the meal. (Make it fun, not perfect!) There is something so special about working together in the kitchen. Everyone should have a job, even Dad! When one is peeling the potatoes and another is making the salad, it is so sweet!

Eat at the table as often as you can. It does take extra effort, but the benefits are so worth it. Today many people know that family mealtimes are important, but many don't realize the full benefits of sharing time together over a meal around the dinner table.

My heart for the Family Dinner is so strong because it has made my family so much closer. When I think back to what sets our family apart, it is the fact that we had dinner at the dinner table almost nightly. Although now my children are adults and have families of their own, they love coming together for our family dinners. That is priceless to me! Meals together around the table are ultimately the recipe for building strong, lifelong family relationships that develop naturally as families share not just a meal, but also the preparation of it and clean-up-together.

I hope you will experience the joy of my life, cooking for the family. Enjoy!

Janet

Helpful Hints

Measurements 10

Kitchen Tools 11

Pantry Items 12

Kids in the Kitchen 13

Measurements

Pan Substitute

If recipe calls for:	You can substitute for:
One 8" x 4" x 2"	Two 5½" x 3¼" loaf pans
One 9" round cake pan	One 8" square pan
Two 9" round cake pans	Three 8" round cake pans
One 13" x 9" x 2" pan	Two 9" round cake pans
One 12-cup fluted tube pan	Two 9" round or 5" x 3" loaf pans

Ledger for measurements

tsp. = teaspoon

Tbs. = tablespoon

lb. = pound

lbs. = pounds

pt. = pint

lt. = liter

pkg. = package

lg. = large

med. = medium

sm. = small

Kitchen Tools

- 1 qt. baking dish
- 2 9" round cake pans
- 2 qt. baking dish
- 9" x 13" baking dish
- Aprons for children
- Breadmaker
- Can opener
- Canisters
- Cookie scoops
- Cutting board for raw meat
- Deep fryer
- Electric skillet
- Food processor
- Garlic press
- Grater
- Hand mixer
- Ice cream scooper
- Kitchen scissors
- Flat measuring cups
- Measuring spoons, liquid & dry
- Meat thermometer
- Mitts
- Mixing bowls, variety of sizes
- Plastic containers
- Muffin pan
- Wooden spoon
- Pizza cutter
- Plastic cutting board
- Silverware divider
- 2 9" pie plates
- 2 aprons
- 3 8" round cake pans
- Airtight containers
- Blender
- Bundt pan
- Candy thermometer
- Colander, 2 sizes
- Cookie sheets (2)
- Wire cooling racks
- Dish sponge holder
- Food chopper
- Freezer containers
- Good set of pots and pans
- Griddle
- Hand towels
- Kitchen Aid mixer
- Loaf pan
- Measuring cups, liquid & dry
- Vegetable peeler
- Wire whisk
- Wood cutting board
- Pastry brush
- Tube pan
- Rolling pin
- Pastry cutter
- Set of knives
- Small roasting pan
- Spatula

Great ideas for wedding gifts or birthday gifts!

Helpful Hints

Pantry Items

- Baking powder
- Basil flakes
- Black beans
- Bow tie pasta
- Canned chicken
- Canned veggies
- Cayenne pepper
- Chile powder
- Cornstarch
- Cream of chicken soup
- Cream of tartar
- Diced tomatoes
- Elbow macaroni
- Flour
- Garlic salt
- Ground cloves
- Ground nutmeg
- Italian seasoning
- Lemon pepper
- Onion salt
- Paprika
- Parsley flakes
- Pinto beans
- Red pepper flakes
- Seasoning salt
- Spaghetti noodles
- Taco seasoning
- Tomato sauce
- Unsweetened cocoa powder
- White pepper

- Baking soda
- Beef bouillon
- Black pepper
- Brown sugar
- Butter flavor Crisco
- Canned fruit
- Canola oil
- Chicken bouillon
- Cooking spray
- Cream of celery soup
- Cream of mushroom soup
- Dill
- Fettuccine noodles
- Garlic powder
- Ground cinnamon
- Ground ginger
- Honey
- Jelly
- Olive oil
- Oregano flakes
- Whole cloves
- Peanut butter
- Powdered sugar
- Salt (sea)
- Self-rising flour
- Sugar
- Thyme
- Tuna
- Vanilla
- White rice

Helpful Hints

Kids in the Kitchen

Shaving cream: Spray inexpensive shaving cream on the kitchen counter and let kids play with Hot Wheel cars and other toys. Cookie cutters work well also. They can have a snow day on the counter! This also cleans the counter top!

Play Dough:

2 cups boiling water

Food coloring

3 tbsp. vegetable oil

Mix all together

In large bowl, combine 2½ cups flour

1 tbsp. Alum

½ cup salt

Pour boiling water mixture over flour mixture. Mix, cool slightly, and knead well. Store in air tight container or plastic bag. Use cookie cutters to play with play dough.

Use different colors to go with seasons of the year. Also you can add in flavoring to make it smell good. It is not edible so don't make it too tempting.

Make **flour dough** and let kids make snacks and other things with it. When they are finished playing, sprinkle the dough with cinnamon and sugar and bake for 8 to 10 minutes for the kid's snacks.

Babies love **the plastic ware cabinet**. Open and they will pull it all out and then climb in. This occupies them while you are cooking.

Pots and pans are great for the kids' first band!

Peanut butter and jelly sandwiches cut out with cookie cutters **make fun snacks** for holidays.

NOTES

Appetizers & Sauces

Baked Hot Wings	17
Cheese Ball	17
Cocktail Sauce	18
Creamy Onion Dip (light)	18
Deviled Eggs	19
French Onion Dip	19
Fruit Dip	20
Fruit Kabobs	20
Garlic and Chile Sauce	21
Guacamole Dip	22
Ham Mustard Glaze	22
Meat & Veggie Egg Rolls	23
Simple Sweet & Sour Sauce	23
Parmesan Chicken Appetizer	24
Pinecone Log	24
Taco Dip	25
Tartar Sauce	25
Traditional Meatballs	26
White Chocolate Party Mix	27

NOTES

Baked Hot Wings

SERVINGS 8–10 • PREP TIME 15 minutes • COOK TIME 40 minutes

- 3 lbs. chicken wings
- 3 eggs, beaten
- 1½ cups cornstarch
- 1 Tbs. baking powder
- ½ tsp. black pepper
- ½ tsp. garlic salt
- ½ tsp. seasoning salt
- 1 bottle hot wing sauce

1 Cut chicken wings into thirds. Discard tips.

2 Place beaten eggs in shallow bowl. Combine seasonings in lg. plastic bag. Dip chicken wings, a few at a time, into eggs and then place in the bag. Shake the bag well to coat. Place coated wings onto a cookie sheet that has been sprayed with cooking spray. Continue until all wings are coated. Spray wings with cooking spray.

3 Bake at 375° F. for 25 minutes.

4 Remove from oven. Using a fresh plastic bag, place a few wings in bag and add some wing sauce. Shake to coat well, return wings to cookie sheet. Continue until all wings are coated. Bake another 15 minutes.

Cheese Ball

SERVINGS 6–8 • PREP TIME 15 minutes • COOK TIME 0 minutes

- 1 lg. pkg. cream cheese, softened
- ½ cup sour cream
- 2 sm. pkg. thinly sliced deli beef
- ½ pkg. dry onion soup mix
- Variety of crackers or breads

1 Combine cream cheese and sour cream.

2 Chop beef in blender until very fine in texture.

3 Add beef and soup mix to the cream cheese and sour cream mixture.

Make one day ahead. Serve with breads or crackers.

Appetizers & Sauces

Cocktail Sauce

SERVINGS vary • PREP TIME 10 minutes • COOK TIME 0 minutes

- 1 cup ketchup
- ¼ cup water
- ¼ cup Mexican Hot Style Tomato sauce
- 1 tsp. crushed red pepper
- 1 tsp. cayenne powder

1 Whisk all ingredients together and serve with your favorite seafood.

Creamy Onion Dip (light)

SERVINGS 2 ½ cups • PREP TIME 5 minutes • COOK TIME 0 minutes

- 2 cups light sour cream
- ½ cup light mayo
- 1 pkg. dry onion soup mix

1 Combine all ingredients in med. serving bowl.

2 Chill for 2 hours or overnight.

Serve with chips or fresh cut veggies.

> *Baking Powder test: To see if your baking powder is still fresh, add 1 tsp. to 1 cup of warm water. If it starts to bubble, you're good to go. If not, throw it out.*

Appetizers & Sauces

Deviled Eggs

SERVINGS 8 (3 per serving) • PREP TIME 25 minutes • COOK TIME 5 minutes

- 12 lg. eggs
- ½ cup mayonnaise
- ¼ cup sweet relish
- 2 Tbs. yellow mustard
- ½ tsp. salt
- ¼ tsp. black pepper
- paprika

1 Place eggs gently into lg. pan. Add cold water to cover all eggs well. On med. high heat, bring to boil. Boil for 5 minutes. Cover pot securely with lid. Turn off heat, leaving pot on burner. Let eggs sit for 20 minutes in hot water.

2 Remove eggs and place in lg. bowl of water with several lg. ice cubes for 10 minutes. Now eggs will peel nicely!

3 Peel eggs and set aside.

4 Slice eggs lengthwise; drop the yolks into a med. bowl. Place halved whites on a serving tray.

5 Combine remaining ingredients, except paprika. Using a pastry knife or fork, smash yokes until slightly creamy and add to mixture in the bowl.

6 Spoon some yolk mixture into each egg white. A cookie press works well for filling the whites. Sprinkle with paprika for garnish. Chill until serving.

French Onion Dip

SERVINGS vary • PREP TIME 0 minutes • COOK TIME 0 minutes

- 2 Tbs. Grandmother's Sunday Roast Seasoning
- 8 oz. sour cream
- Fresh veggies, chips, or crackers

1 Blend seasoning and sour cream well. Chill for 1-2 hours.

2 Serve with chips, crackers, and/or your choice fresh vegetables.

Appetizers & Sauces

Fruit Dip

SERVINGS vary • PREP TIME 20 minutes • COOK TIME 0 minutes

- 8 oz. pkg. cream cheese
- ¾ cup brown sugar
- 8 oz. sour cream
- 2 tsp. vanilla
- 2 tsp. lemon juice
- 1 cup cold water
- 1 3 oz. pkg. instant vanilla pudding

1 In lg. bowl, beat cream cheese and sugar until smooth. Add ingredients one by one, beating well after each addition.

2 Cover and chill 1 hour before serving.

3 Chill 1 hour. Serve with sliced fruit.

Fruit Kabobs

SERVINGS 8 • PREP TIME 30 minutes • COOK TIME 0 minutes

- 1 cup watermelon cubes or balls
- 1 cup cantaloupe cubes or balls
- 1 cup fresh pineapple chunks
- 2 apples
- 2 oranges
- 1 cup strawberries
- ½ cup blueberries
- 8 kabob sticks

1 Cut fruit into bite sized pieces.

2 Thread fruit onto kabob sticks, using some of each fruit.

3 Place on serving tray. Chill until ready to eat.

Appetizers & Sauces

Garlic and Chile Sauce

SERVINGS vary • PREP TIME 15 minutes • COOK TIME 7 minutes

- 4 lg. eggs
- 3 Tbs. butter
- 3 Tbs. all-purpose flour
- 1 cup boiling water
- 8 garlic cloves, peeled
- salt and pepper to taste
- ½ cup olive oil
- 6 sprigs total of fresh parsley, thyme, oregano, chervil, tarragon, chopped
- 2 fresh, med. hot, red chili peppers, rinsed, cored, seeded, ribs removed, divided
- 2 Tbs. tomato paste

1. Boil eggs for 5 minutes at rapid boil, then turn off heat and let sit on burner 20 minutes. Place eggs in lg. bowl of ice water for 10 minutes. Peel eggs and separate yolks from whites; discard whites.

2. Melt butter in saucepan. Whisk in flour and cook 1 minute, or until foaming.

3. Remove pan from heat and whisk in boiling water until sauce thickens. Return to heat and whisk while cooking 1 minute more.

4. Transfer sauce to food processor and add garlic, cooked yolks, salt, and pepper. Puree until smooth. Add oil very slowly in a thin stream through feed tube as processor runs, until sauce is creamy.

5. Add seasonings, peppers, and tomato paste to taste. Store sauce in a bowl or jar in the refrigerator.

Serve appetizers on large lazy Susan in center of table.

Appetizers & Sauces

Guacamole Dip

SERVINGS 4 cups • PREP TIME 20 minutes • COOK TIME 0 minutes

- 5 ripe avocados *
- 2 tomatoes, finely diced
- ½ red onion, finely diced
- ¼ cup cilantro leaves, chopped
- 1 cup Monterey Jack cheese, shredded
- 1 Tbs. lemon juice
- 1 Tbs. seasoning salt
- 1 tsp. garlic salt
- 3 serrano peppers, finely diced
- corn chips

1. Cut avocados lengthwise, remove pit, and spoon out centers into a bowl. Use a pastry knife or fork to smash avocados well.

2. Mix all ingredients in lg. bowl. Serve with corn chips.

3. Store in airtight container. Dip will brown as it sits. Just stir before using.

*Avocados should be dark in color and tender when you squeeze them. If avocados are not ripe, store in paper bag on countertop until softened.

Ham Mustard Glaze

SERVINGS 1 cup • PREP TIME 5 minutes • COOK TIME 0 minutes

- ½ cup yellow mustard
- ½ cup orange marmalade
- ½ tsp. ground ginger

1. Combine ingredients and whisk well. Brush onto ham during last hour of baking. Makes about 1 cup, enough for a 10 to 15 lbs. ham.

Meat & Veggie Egg Rolls

SERVINGS 32 egg rolls • PREP TIME 30 minutes • COOK TIME 30 minutes

- 1 lg. head of cabbage, finely shredded
- 1 lb. bean sprouts
- 1 bunch green onions, chopped
- 1 lb. ground beef
- 1 lb. ground sausage
- 2 eggs
- ½ tsp. ginger
- 2 Tbs. soy sauce
- 1 egg
- 2 pkgs. egg roll wrappers
- Oil for frying

1 Combine all ingredients through soy sauce.

2 In small bowl, beat 1 egg slightly.

3 Place 2-3 tbsp. of meat mixture into the center of egg roll wrapper. Fold wrapper in on the two outsides; using a fingertip, dip finger into beaten egg and then rub the edge of egg roll. Roll over the other direction, seal with more egg "glue." Make sure roll is tight. Set aside. Repeat process with remaining egg rolls.

4 Heat enough oil in lg. skillet to cover 4 to 6 egg rolls. Cook until egg rolls are golden brown on all sides. Continue with remaining egg rolls.

5 Any leftover egg rolls can be frozen after they have cooled. Place on cookie sheet and freeze overnight. Once frozen, place in airtight freezer container or bag. To reheat, place on cookie sheet in oven at 350° F for 20 minutes or microwave for 2 minutes. (Microwaving will not produce crisp egg rolls.)

Simple Sweet & Sour Sauce

SERVINGS 1 cup • PREP TIME 5 minutes • COOK TIME 0 minutes

- ½ cup ketchup
- ½ cup honey

1 Whisk ketchup and honey together and serve with egg rolls.

Appetizers & Sauces

Parmesan Chicken Appetizer

SERVINGS vary • PREP TIME 15 minutes • COOK TIME 15 minutes

- ½ cup club crackers, crushed
- ¼ cup grated Parmesan cheese
- 1 tsp. onion powder
- ½ Tbs. dried parsley flakes
- ¼ tsp. garlic powder
- ⅛ tsp. black pepper
- 2 Tbs. butter
- 3 boneless chicken breasts, cut into strips

1 Preheat oven to 425°. Combine cracker crumbs, cheese, and seasonings in a bowl.

2 Melt butter in a shallow bowl.

3 Dip chicken strips in melted butter, then roll in crumb mixture. Place on lg. cookie sheet that has been sprayed with cooking spray.

4 Sprinkle chicken with remaining crumb mixture. Bake for 15 minutes. Serve with ranch dressing or BBQ sauce for dipping.

Pinecone Log

SERVINGS vary • PREP TIME 10 minutes • COOK TIME 0 minutes

- 8 oz. pkg. cream cheese
- ½ cup mayonnaise
- 5 bacon strips, cooked and crumbled
- 1 Tbs. green onion, finely chopped
- ½ tsp. dried dill
- ⅛ tsp. black pepper
- 1½ cups whole, unblanched almonds, toasted
- Fresh rosemary sprigs
- Assorted crackers or vegetables

1 In lg. bowl, combine first 6 ingredients. Chill 2 hours.

2 Form into 2 pineapple-shaped logs and place on serving platter.

3 Beginning at the narrow end of log, place almonds point side down toward you, stack into overlapping rows.

4 Garnish each log with rosemary sprigs. Serve with crackers or vegetables.

Appetizers & Sauces

Taco Dip

SERVINGS 8–10 • PREP TIME 20 minutes • COOK TIME 10 minutes

- 1 8 oz. pkg. cream cheese, softened
- 8 oz. sour cream
- 1 pkg. dry onion soup mix
- 1 lb. ground beef
- 2 Tbs. diced onion
- 1 pkg. taco seasoning
- 1 can refried beans
- 2 tomatoes, diced
- shredded lettuce
- chopped green bell pepper
- diced black olives
- 1 can whole, pitted black olives
- shredded cheddar cheese
- corn chips
- salsa

1 Blend cream cheese, sour cream and soup mix in lg. bowl. Spread over lg. serving platter and refrigerate, covered, overnight.

2 Brown ground beef with diced onion. Drain well. Add taco seasoning and heat while stirring. Add a little water if needed so it is not dry. Spread over cream cheese mixture on platter.

3 Spread refried beans on top of beef. Top with tomatoes, lettuce, diced olives, and bell pepper.

4 Chill overnight. Sprinkle cheese over the top. Garnish with whole olives around edges of platter. Serve with corn chips and salsa.

Tartar Sauce

SERVINGS 1¼ cups • PREP TIME 5 minutes • COOK TIME 0 minutes

- 1 cup mayonnaise
- 3 Tbs. sweet pickle relish
- 1 Tbs. sugar
- ½ tsp. lemon juice

1 Whisk all ingredients together and refrigerate. The sauce will last a couple of weeks in the refrigerator.

Appetizers & Sauces

Traditional Meatballs

SERVINGS 40 meatballs • **PREP TIME** 25 minutes • **COOK TIME** 1½ hours

- 1 Tbs. butter
- ⅓ cup onion, minced
- 1 lb. ground beef
- ¼ lb. ground pork
- ½ cup saltine crackers, finely crushed
- 1 tsp. cornstarch
- ½ cup milk
- 1 egg
- 1 tsp. nutmeg
- 1 Tbs. sugar
- 1 tsp. salt
- ¼ tsp. black pepper
- parsley
- ¼ cup of ketchup

1 Heat butter and sauté onion in a lg. skillet. Combine remaining ingredients well. (This works great in Kitchen Aid mixer.)

2 Shape into small 1" balls. Brown in same skillet you used for the sauté. Cook on med. heat until cooked through. Remove meatballs and save drippings to make gravy.

Brown Gravy:
- 3 beef bouillon cubes
- 3 cups boiling water
- 5 Tbs. flour
- 1½ tsp. lemon juice
- 3 bay leaves

1 Dissolve bouillon cubes in boiling water. Whisk flour into grease drippings from meatball pan. Add bouillon mixture and whisk until smooth.

2 Add lemon juice and 3 bay leaves and pour gravy with meatballs into an oven safe dish. Bake at 300° F. for 1½ hours. Remove bay leaves before serving. Serve over rice or egg noodles, if desired. You can also use this for meatball sub sandwiches.

Appetizers & Sauces

White Chocolate Party Mix

SERVINGS 20 (½ cup servings) • PREP TIME 15 minutes • COOK TIME 1 hour

- 2 cups powdered sugar
- 2 Tbs. unsweetened cocoa powder
- ½ cup butter, melted
- 4 cups Cheerios
- 4 cups Wheat Chex
- 1 cup slivered almonds
- 1 cup raisins
- 12 oz. white chocolate chips

1. In small bowl, combine sugar and cocoa. Stir in butter.

2. In lg. bowl, combine cereals and almonds.

3. Pour butter mixture over cereal and toss to coat well.

4. Spread on 9" x 13" cookie sheet. Bake at 250° F. for 1 hour, stirring every 15 minutes. Cool completely.

5. Stir in raisins and chocolate chips. Store in airtight container.

To toast coconut or nuts, bake at 375° F. for 5 to 7 minutes, stirring occasionally until golden brown.

Appetizers & Sauces

Breads & Breakfasts

Apple Banana Bread	31
Apricot Cranberry Bread	32
Banana Bread	31
Blueberry Buckle	33
Breakfast Burritos	33
Caramel Breakfast Rolls	34
Cheesy Garlic Biscuits	34
Chocolate and Biscuits	35
Chocolate Sour Cream Coffee Cake	36
Cinnamon Rolls	37
Coffee Cake	38
Corn Bread	35
Cranberry Nut Muffins	41
Crescent Rolls	39
Dinner Rolls	40
Easy Drop Danish	41
French Breakfast Muffins	42
Gingerbread	43
Lemon Bread	37
Monkey Bread	45
Pancakes & Waffles	44
Pumpkin Bread	45
Rhubarb-Pecan Muffins	46
Sausage Quiche	46
Streusel Topping	38
Zucchini Bread	47

NOTES

Apple Banana Bread

SERVINGS 2 loaves • PREP TIME 10 minutes • COOK TIME 1 hour

- ½ cup margarine
- 2 cups sugar
- 2 eggs
- 4 apples, finely chopped
- 3 lg. bananas, mashed
- 2 tsp. vanilla

- 2 cups all purpose flour
- 2 tsp. baking powder
- 2 tsp. baking soda
- ½ tsp. salt
- 1 cup raisins (optional)
- 1 cup walnuts (optional)

1 Preheat oven to 325° F. Cream margarine. Add sugar, then eggs, beating after each addition.

2 Stir in apples and bananas. Add vanilla.

3 Sift together flour, baking powder, baking soda, and salt, then add to batter.

4 Stir until well blended.

5 Grease and flour two loaf pans. Pour half of batter into each pan.

6 Bake for 1 hour.

Banana Bread

SERVINGS 8–10 • PREP TIME 10 minutes • COOK TIME 1 hour

- ½ cup shortening
- 1 cup sugar
- 2 eggs
- 1½ cups mashed bananas

- 1½ Tbs. sour milk
- 1 tsp. lemon juice
- 2 cups self-rising flour
- 1 cup chopped nuts (optional)

1 Preheat oven to 350° F. Cream shortening with sugar and beat in eggs until light.

2 Add bananas, milk, and lemon juice. Mix well.

3 Bake in greased loaf pan for 1 hour or until done.

Breads & Breakfasts

Apricot Cranberry Bread

SERVINGS one loaf • **PREP TIME** 10 minutes • **COOK TIME** 1 hour

- 2 cups self-rising flour
- 1 cup sugar
- 2 tsp. grated orange peel
- ½ tsp. sea salt
- 1 egg
- ¾ cup water
- ¼ cup vegetable oil
- 1 cup fresh or frozen cranberries
- ¼ cup apricot preserves

1 Preheat oven to 350° F. In lg. bowl, combine first 4 ingredients.

2 In smaller bowl, beat egg, oil, and water.

3 Stir wet mixture into dry ingredients until moist. Fold in cranberries.

4 Grease and flour a 9" x 5" x 3" loaf pan. Spread batter in pan.

5 Cut apricots into small pieces and spread over batter. Take a butter knife and swirl preserves into batter.

6 Bake for 60 to 70 minutes. Test with toothpick, piecing the center of the bread. Bread is done when toothpick comes out clean.

7 Cool for 10 minutes, then place on wire rack to completely cool.

> Baking Powder test: To see if your baking powder is still fresh, add 1 tsp. to 1 cup of warm water. If it starts to bubble, you're good to go, if not, throw it out.

Breads & Breakfasts

Blueberry Buckle

SERVINGS 12 • PREP TIME 10 minutes • COOK TIME 1 hour, 15 minutes

- ½ cup butter
- ½ cup granulated sugar
- 1 egg, slightly beaten
- 2 cups self-rising flour
- ½ cup milk
- 2 cups fresh blueberries, washed, or frozen, thawed
- ¼ cup butter
- ½ cup granulated sugar
- ½ cup flour
- ½ tsp. ground cinnamon

1 Preheat oven to 350°. Spray 8" x 8" x 2" baking dish with cooking spray; set aside.

2 Cream butter and ½ cup sugar; add egg and mix well.

3 Add flour alternately with milk. Spread into prepared dish.

4 Spread blueberries over the top of batter.

5 Combine remaining ingredients by cutting in the butter until crumbly. Sprinkle over top of blueberries.

6 Bake for 1 hour and 15 minutes.

Breakfast Burritos

SERVINGS 4 • PREP TIME 15 minutes • COOK TIME 10 minutes

- 2 cups frozen shredded hash browns
- 4 lg. flour tortillas
- 6 eggs, scrambled
- 3 bacon strips, cooked and crumbled
- 2 green onions, finely chopped
- 1 cup shredded cheese
- 1 20 oz. can green chili sauce

1 Cook hash browns until golden brown in a little bit of hot oil.

2 On each tortilla, place some eggs, bacon, onion, hash browns, and then cheese.

3 Add a lg. spoonful of green chili sauce over the cheese.

4 Roll up like a burrito and heat in microwave for about 1 minute each. Pour any remaining sauce over heated burritos, if desired.

Caramel Breakfast Rolls

SERVINGS 8–10 • PREP TIME 10 minutes, plus overnight
COOK TIME 30 minutes

- 1 pkg. frozen dinner rolls
- ½ cup melted butter
- 3 oz. butterscotch pudding (not instant)
- 1 cup chopped pecans
- ½ cup brown sugar
- 1½ tsp. cinnamon

1 Spray Bundt pan with cooking spray. Place frozen rolls in pan.

2 Pour melted butter over rolls.

3 Mix remaining ingredients and sprinkle over rolls. Cover with cake dome; let rise overnight. Dough will rise over height of pan.

4 Bake at 350° for 25 to 30 minutes. Immediately turn out on platter and serve while warm.

5 If desired, drizzle icing over warm rolls before serving.

Icing drizzle: 1½ cups powdered sugar, ½ tsp. vanilla, few drops of milk. Whisk together, adding milk until right consistency. Icing should be thin enough to drizzle.

Cheesy Garlic Biscuits

SERVINGS 12 • PREP TIME 5 minutes • COOK TIME 10 minutes

- 2 cups Bisquick
- ⅔ cup milk
- ½ cup shredded cheese
- 2 Tbs. melted butter
- ⅛ tsp. garlic powder

1 Preheat oven to 450° F. Mix first 3 ingredients to form soft dough.

2 Drop by spoonfuls onto ungreased cookie sheet.

3 Bake 10 minutes or until golden brown.

4 Mix butter and garlic in small bowl; brush over warm biscuits.

Breads & Breakfasts

Chocolate and Biscuits

SERVINGS 4 • PREP TIME 5 minutes • COOK TIME 15 minutes

- 1 can lg. biscuits
- ¼ cup unsweetened Hershey's cocoa
- ¼ cup milk
- ¾ cup sugar
- 2 Tbs. butter
- ¼ tsp. vanilla

1 Bake biscuits as directed on can.

2 While biscuits are baking, make sauce. Mix cocoa, milk, and sugar in med. saucepan.

3 Stir over med. high heat until bubbly.

4 Add butter and turn off heat. Add vanilla and stir well.

5 Pour over hot biscuits.

Corn Bread

SERVINGS 8 • PREP TIME 10 minutes • COOK TIME 25 minutes

- 1 cup flour
- ¼ cup sugar
- 4 tsp. baking powder
- ¾ tsp. salt
- 1 cup yellow cornmeal
- 2 eggs
- 1 cup milk
- ¾ cup shortening

1 Preheat oven to 425° F. Combine flour, sugar, baking powder, and salt. Stir in cornmeal.

2 Add eggs, milk, and shortening; beat for 1 minute on med. speed.

3 Pour batter into greased 9" x 9" x 2" pan, or lined muffin pan.

4 Bake for 25 minutes. Serve with butter.

Chocolate Sour Cream Coffee Cake

SERVINGS 8–10 • PREP TIME 25 minutes • COOK TIME 60–90 minutes

Cake:
- 1 cup butter, softened
- 2 cups granulated sugar
- 2 eggs
- 2 cups self-rising flour
- 1 cup sour cream
- ½ tsp. vanilla

Topping:
- 1 cup chopped pecans
- 2 Tbs. granulated sugar
- 1 tsp. cinnamon

Chocolate Glaze:
- ½ cup semisweet chocolate chips
- ¼ cup butter

1. Preheat oven to 350° F. In lg. mixing bowl, combine butter and sugar. Beat until fluffy. Add eggs and beat until smooth. Gradually add flour, blending well. Gently fold in sour cream and vanilla—do not beat.

2. For topping, combine ingredients in a small mixing bowl. Set aside.

3. For glaze, melt chocolate chips and butter in small saucepan over low heat, stirring until smooth.

4. Grease and flour tube pan. Sprinkle 2 Tbs. topping mixture on bottom of tube pan.

5. Spoon half of batter onto topping in pan. Sprinkle 4 Tbs. of topping over batter and drizzle half of the glaze over topping.

6. Spoon remaining batter over glaze and sprinkle with remaining topping mixture. Reserve remaining glaze.

7. Bake for 1 hour to 90 minutes. Insert lg. toothpick into center of cake to test if done. Cool in pan 10 minutes.

8. Transfer to serving platter with nut side up. Warm remaining glaze and drizzle over the top before serving.

Let company help you cook or set the table. People like a job to do so they are not uncomfortable.

Breads & Breakfasts

Cinnamon Rolls

SERVINGS 8 • PREP TIME 10 minutes • COOK TIME 15 minutes

- ¾ cup packed brown sugar
- ¼ cup flour
- 1 Tbs. cinnamon
- ⅓ cup butter
- 1 can Pillsbury Grands Biscuits

Frosting:
- 3 oz. cream cheese
- ¼ cup butter
- 4 cups powdered sugar
- ½ tsp. vanilla
- milk

1 Preheat oven to 400° F. Mix all ingredients except biscuits. Cut butter into flour mixture using a pastry cutter or two table knives. Mixture will be crumbly.

2 Roll out each biscuit on floured surface until ¼" thick. Spread some cinnamon mixture on biscuits. Roll up, cut in half using dental floss. Place in a pie pan sprayed with cooking spray. Continue with each biscuit the same way.

3 Bake for 15 minutes.

4 Mix cream cheese and ¼ cup butter. Add powdered sugar, vanilla, and a few drops of milk. Blend; frosting will be a thick consistency. Spread over hot cinnamon rolls right out of the oven.

Lemon Bread

SERVINGS 6–8 • PREP TIME 10 minutes • COOK TIME 1 hour

- 1 cup oil
- 1½ cups sugar
- ¼ tsp. salt
- 6 eggs
- 2 tsp. baking powder
- ⅔ cup flour
- 2 lemons, grated
- ½ cup nuts
- powdered sugar

1 Preheat oven to 300° F. Beat oil, sugar, salt, and lemon peel. Add eggs one at a time; beat after each egg.

2 Sift baking powder and flour together.

3 Add to oil mixture. Add nuts.

4 Bake in 2 greased 9" x 5" x 3" pans for 1 hour.

5 Sprinkle with powdered sugar immediately after baking.

Breads & Breakfasts

Coffee Cake

SERVINGS 8–10 • PREP TIME 10 minutes • COOK TIME 42–45 minutes

- 2 cups sifted flour
- ½ tsp. salt
- 1 tsp. baking soda
- 1 tsp. baking powder
- ¼ Tbs. butter
- 1 cup sugar
- 2 eggs
- ½ pkg. sour cream
- ½ tsp. almond extract

Topping:
- ½ cup sugar
- 1 tsp. cinnamon
- ½ cup chopped nuts

1. Preheat oven to 375° F. Sift together flour, salt, baking soda, and baking powder.
2. Cream butter and sugar. Add eggs one at a time.
3. Add flour mixture to creamed mixture. Add sour cream, almond extract.
4. Grease an angel food cake pan. Place half of batter into pan.
5. Mix sugar, cinnamon, and nuts. Sprinkle half over batter.
6. Add remaining batter, then remaining cinnamon sugar.
7. Bake for 42 to 45 minutes.

Streusel Topping

SERVINGS 12 muffins • PREP TIME 5 minutes • COOK TIME 0 minutes

- 3 Tbs. flour
- 2 Tbs. brown sugar
- ½ tsp. cinnamon
- ½ cup chopped nuts (optional)
- 3 Tbs. butter

1. Combine all except butter in a small bowl.
2. Cut in butter with a pastry knife until crumbly.
3. Use to top muffins or coffee cake before baking.

Breads & Breakfasts

Crescent Rolls

SERVINGS 12 • PREP TIME 10 minutes, overnight, then two hours rising • COOK TIME 8–10 minutes

- 1 cup scalded milk
- ½ cup sugar
- ½ tsp. baking soda
- 1 pkg. yeast, softened in ¼ cup of water
- ½ cup oil
- 1 tsp. salt
- 2 eggs
- 4 cups all-purpose flour

1 Mix all ingredients, beating after each addition.

2 Cover bowl with plastic wrap. Leave at room temperature overnight.

3 Turn out onto floured surface and knead. Divide into 3 parts.

4 Roll each part in a circle. Cut each circle in 12 pie-piece shaped wedges.

5 Starting with wide edge, roll up each piece into a crescent.

6 Place on greased cookie sheet 1 inch apart. Cover and let rise 2 hours or longer.

7 Bake at 350° F. 8 to 10 minutes or until golden brown. These rolls are very light and fluffy. They also can be rolled out earlier and formed and left to rise at room temperature.

To scald is to heat just before boiling and tiny bubbles begin to form on the edge of sauce pan.

Breads & Breakfasts

Dinner Rolls

**SERVINGS 12–15 • PREP TIME 15 minutes, 70 minutes rising
COOK TIME 20 minutes**

- 3 cups all-purpose flour, divided
- 2 Tbs. sugar
- 1 pkg. dry active yeast
- 1 tsp. salt
- 1 cup water
- 2 Tbs. butter
- 1 egg
- 2 Tbs. melted butter

1 Combine 2 cups flour, sugar, yeast, and salt in mixing bowl.

2 In med. saucepan, heat water and 2 Tbs. butter to 130°, according to a cooking thermometer. Add dry ingredients; beat until blended.

3 Add egg; beat on low for 30 seconds, then beat on high for 3 minutes. Stir in remaining flour. Do not knead.

4 Cover and let rise at room temperature for 30 minutes or until doubled in size. Stir dough down and place in muffin cups about half full.

5 Cover and let rise 40 minutes.

6 Bake at 350° F. for 15 to 20 minutes or until golden brown.

7 Cool 1 minute before removing to wire rack. Brush tops with melted butter.

Make double portions as often as possible and freeze one of them.

Breads & Breakfasts

Easy Drop Danish

SERVINGS 12–15 • PREP TIME 10 minutes • COOK TIME 15 minutes

- 2 cups Bisquick
- ¼ cup margarine, softened
- 2 Tbs. sugar
- ⅔ cup milk
- Jam, any flavor

Glaze:
- ⅔ cup powdered sugar
- 1 Tbs. warm water
- ¼ tsp. vanilla

1. Preheat oven to 450° F. Mix Bisquick, margarine, and sugar until crumbly.
2. Stir in milk until dough forms.
3. Drop by rounded Tbs. about 2 inches apart onto lightly greased cookie sheet.
4. Make a shallow well in center of each Danish and fill with 1 tsp. jam.
5. Bake 10 to 15 minutes. Combine glaze ingredients and drizzle over Danishes while warm.

Cranberry Nut Muffins

SERVINGS 12 • PREP TIME 5 minutes • COOK TIME 18-22 minutes

- ¼ cup sugar
- 2 eggs, slightly beaten
- ½ cup light corn syrup
- ½ cup milk
- ¼ cup oil
- 1 tsp. grated orange peel
- 1½ cups self-rising flour
- 1 cup cranberries
- ½ cup chopped walnuts

1. Preheat oven to 400° F. Line muffin tin with paper liners; spray papers with cooking spray.
2. In mixing bowl, combine sugar, eggs, corn syrup, milk, oil, and orange peel. Mix well. Stir in flour until moist.
3. Stir in cranberries and walnuts; mix well. Spoon batter into muffin cups. Bake 18 to 22 minutes. Cool 5 minutes in pan.

Breads & Breakfasts

French Breakfast Muffins

SERVINGS 12 • PREP TIME 10 minutes • COOK TIME 25 minutes

- ⅓ cup shortening
- ½ cup sugar
- 1 egg
- ½ cup milk
- ¼ tsp. nutmeg
- ½ tsp. vanilla

- 1½ cups self-rising flour

Topping:
- ½ cup melted butter
- ½ cup sugar
- 1 tsp. ground cinnamon

1 Preheat oven to 350° F. Prepare muffin pan with paper liners* or spray with cooking spray.

2 In lg. mixing bowl, combine shortening and sugar.

3 Add egg, vanilla, and milk.

4 Stir nutmeg into flour. Add flour mixture to creamed mixture. Mix well.

5 Spoon mixture into lightly greased muffin cups.

6 Bake for 25 minutes.

7 In smaller bowl, combine topping ingredients.

8 When muffins are done and still warm, slightly dip the top of each muffin into the topping mixture. Serve warm.

*Spray paper liners to prevent sticking.

A Kitchen Aid mixer works well to mash potatoes or knead dough.

Breads & Breakfasts

Gingerbread

SERVINGS one loaf • **PREP TIME** 10 minutes • **COOK TIME** 30–35 minutes

- 1 cup butter, softened
- 1 cup sugar
- 3 eggs
- 1 cup dark molasses
- ¾ cup hot water
- 2½ cups self-rising flour

- 1½ tsp. ground ginger
- 1 tsp. ground cinnamon
- 1 tsp. ground nutmeg
- ½ tsp. salt
- 1 cup whipping cream
- 2 Tbs. powdered sugar

1 Preheat oven to 350° F. Spray 9" x 13" baking dish with cooking spray and set aside.

2 In lg. mixing bowl, combine butter and sugar; beat for 3 minutes on low.

3 Add eggs; beat on low for 2 minutes. Gradually add molasses and hot water.

4 Combine flour, ginger, cinnamon, nutmeg and salt in med. bowl. Gradually add to creamed mixture. Beat on low 1 minute to blend well.

5 Spread into prepared pan. Bake for 30 to 35 minutes. Test with toothpick in center of cake. Cool on wire rack.

6 For topping, beat whipping cream and powdered sugar until peaks form. Serve on gingerbread. Sprinkle with ground nutmeg for decoration.

Breads freeze for a long time in freezer bags. Mark and date them.

Breads & Breakfasts

Pancakes & Waffles

**SERVINGS 10–12 pancakes • PREP TIME 10 minutes
COOK TIME 15 minutes**

- 2 cups self-rising flour
- 3 Tbs. sugar
- 2 eggs
- 1½ cups milk
- 2 Tbs. oil (for waffles)

For pancakes:

1. Spray griddle with cooking spray; heat to med. high.
2. Combine ingredients in order given. When the griddle is hot, spoon 2 lg. spoons of batter onto griddle to make one lg. pancake. Use smaller amounts for silver dollar-size pancakes.
3. Flip pancakes when the top begins to set and bubbles are starting to appear.

For waffles:

4. Heat waffle iron and spray with cooking spray. Combine ingredients in order given.
5. Spoon batter into the center and close lid. Cook for about 4 minutes or until done.

Variations:
Blueberry: Add blueberries after pouring batter on the griddle or the waffle iron.
Banana Nut: Smash 1 lg. banana and add to batter; fold in ½ cup chopped walnuts.

> *Fried eggs: Spray nonstick pan with cooking spray. When pan is hot, break eggs into pan. Spray top of eggs with cooking spray before flipping. This helps cut calories!*

Breads & Breakfasts

Monkey Bread

SERVINGS 8–10 • PREP TIME 15 minutes • COOK TIME 25 minutes

- 2 cans large biscuits
- ½ cup butter, melted
- 1 tsp. ground cinnamon
- ½ cup chopped pecans
- 1 cup packed brown sugar

1 Preheat oven to 375° F. Cut biscuits into small squares.

2 Combine butter, cinnamon, nuts, and sugar in small bowl.

3 Spray Bundt or tube pan with cooking spray. Pour in butter and spice mixture.

4 Add biscuits, stacking them on each other.

5 Bake for 25 minutes. Remove from oven and immediately invert onto serving plate. Serve warm.

Pumpkin Bread

SERVINGS 6–8 • PREP TIME 10 minutes • COOK TIME 1 hour

- ⅔ cup shortening
- 2⅔ cups sugar
- 4 eggs
- 1 16 oz. can pumpkin
- 3⅓ cup self-rising flour
- ⅔ cup nuts
- ⅔ cup raisins
- 2 tsp. pumpkin pie spice

1 Preheat oven to 350° F. Combine all ingredients in order given. Mix until blended; batter does not need to be smooth.

2 Pour into loaf pan sprayed with cooking spray.

3 Bake for 1 hour. Serve with Cool Whip, if desired.

Rhubarb-Pecan Muffins

SERVINGS 12 • PREP TIME 15 minutes • COOK TIME 30 minutes

- 2 cups self-rising flour
- ¾ cup sugar
- ¼ cup chopped pecans
- 1 egg
- ½ cup oil
- 2 tsp. grated orange peel
- ¾ cup orange juice
- 1¼ cups shredded rhubarb

1. Preheat oven to 350° F. Combine flour, sugar, and nuts in lg. mixing bowl.
2. In another bowl, combine egg, oil, orange peel and orange juice. Mix well.
3. Add wet ingredients to dry ingredients and stir just until moistened. Stir in rhubarb.
4. Line muffin pan with paper liners or spray with cooking spray. Fill each almost to the top.
5. Bake for 25 to 30 minutes.

Sausage Quiche

SERVINGS 6–8 • PREP TIME 15 minutes • COOK TIME 25 minutes

- 1 lb. Italian sausage
- 6 eggs
- ¼ cup milk
- 1 cup shredded cheese
- 2 stalks of green onions, chopped
- salt and pepper
- ready-made pie crust

1. Preheat oven to 400° F. Cook sausage in skillet until cooked through; drain.
2. Mix remaining ingredients with sausage in lg. bowl.
3. Place pie crust into a lg. pie plate and flute edges.
4. Pour egg and sausage mixture into pie crust.
5. Bake for 25 minutes.

Serve with sliced fruit.

Breads & Breakfasts

Zucchini Bread

SERVINGS 2 loaves • **PREP TIME** 15 minutes • **COOK TIME** 1 hour

- 3 eggs
- 1 cup oil
- 2 cups sugar
- 2 cups grated, peeled zucchini
- 3 tsp. vanilla

- 3 cups self-rising flour
- ¼ tsp. nutmeg
- 3 tsp. ground cinnamon
- 1 cup chopped nuts

1 Preheat oven to 350° F. Combine eggs, oil, sugar, zucchini, and vanilla until well blended.

2 Combine flour, nutmeg, and cinnamon in lg. bowl and add to wet ingredients.

3 Stir in chopped nuts.

4 Divide into two loaf pans that have been sprayed with cooking spray.

5 Bake for 1 hour.

Use coconut oil for frying. Coconut oil has many benefits. Research and see if it is something that could benefit you and your family.

Breads & Breakfasts

Beverages

Banana-Orange Honey Shake	51
Cranberry Apple Cider	51
Hot Apple Cider	52
Hot Chocolate Mix	52
Hot Fruit Drink	53
Orange Julius	53
Party Punch	54
Spice Tea Mix	54

Hot chocolate or spice tea mix makes a great gift for teachers any time of year! Use a canning jar with a lid; cut fabric in a square and tie onto lid with a matching ribbon. Kids will love to help with this!

NOTES

Banana-Orange Honey Shake

SERVINGS 6 • PREP TIME 5 minutes • COOK TIME 0 minutes

- 2 oranges, peeled and cut into bite-sized pieces
- 1 banana, peeled and sliced
- ½ cup low-fat or nonfat milk
- 1 egg (optional)
- 1 tsp. honey
- ¼ tsp. vanilla
- 2 ice cubes
- ground nutmeg (optional)

1 Place oranges, banana, milk, egg (if desired), honey, and vanilla in blender or food processor.

2 Cover and blend about 30 seconds or until smooth.

3 With machine running, add ice cubes, one at a time, through hole in lid of blender or feed tube of processor. Blend a few more seconds until smooth.

4 Pour into 3 glasses. Sprinkle with ground nutmeg, if desired.

Cranberry Apple Cider

SERVINGS 16 • PREP TIME 15 minutes • COOK TIME 0 minutes

- 2 qts. apple juice
- 1 cup fresh cranberries, crushed
- 1 med. apple, peeled and thinly sliced
- 1 med. orange, thinly sliced
- 1 cinnamon stick

1 In lg. stock pot or slow cooker, combine all ingredients.

2 Heat to desired temperature and keep warm while serving.

Beverages

Hot Apple Cider

SERVINGS 36 • PREP TIME 15 minutes • COOK TIME 0 minutes

- 12 whole cloves
- 1 orange, thinly sliced
- 4 cinnamon sticks
- 1 tsp. ground nutmeg
- 1 gallon apple juice

1. Press cloves into each orange slice.
2. Place cinnamon sticks, cloves, and nutmeg into a square of cheesecloth and tie to secure.
3. In lg. stock pot, combine all ingredients and bring to a hard boil.
4. Reduce heat and simmer. Keep hot as you serve.

* if you don't have the cheesecloth, strain cider with a sieve before serving.

Hot Chocolate Mix

SERVINGS vary • PREP TIME 10 minutes • COOK TIME 0 minutes

- 2 lbs. can Nestlé's Quik
- 4 cups powdered sugar
- 20 oz. canister powdered coffee creamer
- 15 oz. instant milk

1. Blend ingredients well with a wire whisk.
2. Place in glass jars or small gift bags. Store bags in airtight container.
3. To prepare, add 3 Tbs. hot chocolate mix to 1 cup hot water. This makes great small gifts. Write preparation instructions to accompany jars or bags. Add mini marshmallows to mix if desired.

Hot Fruit Drink

SERVINGS 24 • PREP TIME 10 minutes • COOK TIME 15 minutes

- 1 qt. cranberry cocktail
- 1 sm. can frozen orange juice, reconstituted as directed
- 1 sm. can frozen lemonade concentrate (do not add water)
- ⅓ cup honey
- 2 cinnamon sticks
- 3 whole cloves
- 1 qt. ginger ale

1 Combine all ingredients except ginger ale in lg. kettle; simmer 15 minutes.

2 Add ginger ale before serving.

Orange Julius

SERVINGS 4 • PREP TIME 10 minutes • COOK TIME 0 minutes

- ½ cup frozen orange juice concentrate
- ½ cup milk
- 2 Tbs. honey or sugar
- ¾ tsp. vanilla
- 6 to 8 ice cubes
- Fruit: banana chunks, strawberries, blueberries, etc.

1 Combine orange juice, milk, honey, and vanilla in blender.

2 Add ice cubes one a time as you blend. Blend until smooth.

3 Add fruit and blend until smooth.

Beverages

Party Punch

**SERVINGS 32 • PREP TIME 25 minutes, freeze overnight
COOK TIME 0 minutes**

- 1 can frozen fruit juice, reconstituted as directed
- 2 lt. Sprite® or 7 Up®
- 1 lt. ginger ale
- 1 qt. sherbet

1 Freeze reconstituted fruit juice in ice cube trays or 2 ring molds overnight.

2 About 20 minutes before serving, place ½ the sherbet, and half of each soda in lg. punch bowl.

3 Add frozen juice cubes or molds to bowl. Let stand 20 minutes before serving.

Spice Tea Mix

SERVINGS 4 cups of mix • PREP TIME 10 minutes • COOK TIME 0 minutes

- 2 cups orange Tang®
- 1 pkg. Kool-Aid® lemonade
- 1 cup sugar
- 1 cup unflavored instant tea
- 2 tsp. ground cinnamon
- 2 tsp. ground cloves
- 1 tsp. ground nutmeg

1 Combine ingredients in a lg. bowl.

2 Store in jars or airtight containers. Stir well before each use.

3 To prepare, use 2 to 3 round tsp. for each cup of hot water. Place mix in small 8 oz. jars for gifts for the holidays. Top jars with a 4" x 4" square of Christmas fabric tied with a Christmas ribbon.

Beverages

Salads & Dressings

Broccoli Salad	57
Chicken Salad on Croissants	57
Creamy Celery Seed Dressing	58
Creamy Cranberry Salad	58
Crunchy Tuna Salad	59
Cucumber Salad	59
Egg Salad	60
Fresh Asparagus Salad	60
Fruit Salad	61
Garlicky Lemon Buttermilk Dressing	61
Italian Pasta Salad	62
Jell-O Salad	62
Lemony Chicken Salad	63
Macaroni Salad	63
Oriental Chicken Salad	64
Pear & Walnut Spring Mix Salad	64
Potato Salad	65
Red Wine Vinaigrette Dressing	66
Summer Fruit Salad	66
Summer Special Salad	67
Thousand Island Dressing	67
Tossed Salad with Walnuts & Cranberries	68
Turkey Salad	68

NOTES

Broccoli Salad

SERVINGS 8 • PREP TIME 20 minutes • COOK TIME 1 minute

- 4 cups chopped broccoli
- 4 strips bacon
- ¼ cup onion, chopped
- ½ cup sunflower seeds
- ¼ cup slivered almonds
- ½ cup raisins

Dressing:
- 4 Tbs. sugar
- 6 Tbs. vinegar
- 1½ cups mayonnaise
- 1 tsp. lemon juice
- ½ tsp. each salt, black pepper, and sesame seeds

1 Boil 6 cups of water. Cook broccoli in boiling water for 1 minute.*

2 Cook bacon till crispy and drain on paper towel. Crumble when cool.

3 Combine all ingredients in lg. bowl.

4 Mix all dressing ingredients well.

5 Toss dressing with salad and refrigerate for a couple of hours or overnight.

* Flash cooking the broccoli will open up the heads and bring out the vibrant green color.

Chicken Salad on Croissants

SERVINGS 10–12 • PREP TIME 20 minutes • COOK TIME 20 minutes

- 3 cups cooked, diced chicken
- ½ cup red bell pepper, finely diced
- ¾ cup mayonnaise
- 1 tsp. thyme
- ¼ tsp. each dill, salt, and black pepper

1 Combine all ingredients in lg. bowl. Chill for about 2 hours.

2 Serve over bed of lettuce, wrap in flour tortillas, or fill split croissants.

Salads & Dressings

Creamy Celery Seed Dressing

SERVINGS 1½ cups • PREP TIME 5 minutes • COOK TIME 0 minutes

- 1 cup mayonnaise
- 4 Tbs. vinegar
- 6 Tbs. sugar
- ½ tsp. celery seed
- ½ tsp. lemon juice

1 Mix well with whisk. Store in refrigerator up to 2 weeks.

Creamy Cranberry Salad

SERVINGS 8 • PREP TIME 15 minutes • COOK TIME 0 minutes

- 3 cups fresh or frozen cranberries, chopped
- 1 20 oz. can crushed pineapple, drained
- 1 med. apple, peeled and chopped
- 2 cups mini marshmallows
- ⅔ cup granulated sugar
- ⅛ tsp. salt
- ¼ cup chopped walnuts
- 2 cups whipping cream, whipped

1 In lg. bowl, mix well all ingredients except the whipped cream.

2 Cover and refrigerate overnight.

3 Just before serving, fold in whipped cream.

Crunchy Tuna Salad

SERVINGS 6 • PREP TIME 10 minutes • COOK TIME 0 minutes

- 2 lg. cans tuna in water, drained
- 3 hardboiled eggs, diced
- 2 celery stalks, washed and chopped
- 2 lg. carrots, peeled and chopped
- ½ cup mayonnaise
- ¼ cup sweet pickle relish
- ¼ tsp. salt
- ⅛ tsp. black pepper

1 Combine all ingredients in lg. bowl. Add more mayonnaise if salad is too dry.

2 Place lg. spoonful on your favorite bread or roll. Great on croissants!

Variations:

Tuna Melt Sandwich
Place slice of bread on cookie sheet, spoon tuna onto bread. Top with a slice of Swiss cheese. Bake at 400° F. for 15 minutes or until cheese melts.

Lettuce Wrap
Wash lg. leaves of lettuce and spoon tuna into the middle of each leaf. Roll by wrapping lettuce around tuna and use a toothpick to secure roll.

Cucumber Salad

SERVINGS 4 • PREP TIME 10 minutes • COOK TIME 0 minutes

- 3 cucumbers, partially peeled
- ½ red onion, thinly sliced
- 1 cup cherry tomatoes
- ¼ cup zesty Italian salad dressing

1 Cut cucumbers in half lengthwise. Spoon out seeds. Thinly slice each half..

2 Combine cucumber slices with onion and tomatoes in med. bowl.

3 Toss with salad dressing and chill until ready to serve.

Salads & Dressings

Egg Salad

SERVINGS 4 • PREP TIME 15 minutes • COOK TIME 5 minutes

- 6 hard boiled eggs, chopped
- ½ cup chopped pimento
- ¼ cup chopped green onions
- ½ cup chopped celery
- ½ cup mayonnaise
- 6 lg. tomatoes

1. Combine chopped eggs, pimento, onions, celery, and mayonnaise. Chill about 1 hour.
2. Cut tomatoes stem side down and scoop out seeds. Cut into quarters, but not all the way through, to make a rose-looking bowl.
3. Scoop egg mixture into each tomato and serve.

To hard boil eggs, place in lg. stock pot and cover with water. Bring to full boil for 5 minutes. Turn off heat, leaving pot on hot burner. Cover pot and let sit for 15 minutes. Transfer eggs to bowl of ice water and let sit for 10 minutes. This process will help eggs to peel well.

Fresh Asparagus Salad

SERVINGS 4 • PREP TIME 10 minutes • COOK TIME 5 minutes

- 1 lb. fresh asparagus
- ¼ cup fresh lemon juice
- 2 Tbs. honey
- 1 Tbs. olive oil
- 8 lg. lettuce leaves

1. Trim asparagus and cut off tough ends. Cook in boiling water or steam until barely tender, about 5 minutes.
2. Plunge into ice water. Drain and chill.
3. Combine lemon juice, honey, and oil in a jar and shake well. Chill.
4. Arrange asparagus over lettuce and drizzle with dressing.

Fruit Salad

SERVINGS 8 • PREP TIME 20 minutes • COOK TIME 0 minutes

- 1 apple
- 1 orange, peeled
- 2 cups watermelon
- 1 cup cantaloupe
- 1 cup strawberries
- ½ cup blueberries
- 2 bananas, peeled
- 1 cup finely chopped nuts (optional)
- 1 cup yogurt, any flavor
- 2 cups Cool Whip

1. Chop all fruit into bite-sizes and place in lg. bowl. Toss to mix.
2. In small bowl, combine Cool Whip and yogurt and toss with fruit.
3. Chill until ready to eat.

Garlicky Lemon Buttermilk Dressing

SERVINGS 2½ cups • PREP TIME 5 minutes • COOK TIME 0 minutes

- ¾ cup canola oil
- ½ cup fresh lemon juice
- ½ cup mayonnaise
- ⅓ cup buttermilk
- 4 or 5 garlic cloves, pressed
- 1½ Tbs. dried dill weed
- 1½ Tbs. sugar
- 1½ Tbs. coarsely ground black pepper
- 1 tsp. salt

1. Put all ingredients in a jar with a tight-fitting lid and shake well or whisk thoroughly.
2. Keep refrigerated. Shake well before each use.

Salads & Dressings

Italian Pasta Salad

SERVINGS 6 cups • PREP TIME 10 minutes • COOK TIME 15 minutes

- 1 bag tri-color pasta
- 2 carrots, peeled and thinly sliced
- 1 bunch of broccoli, cut in bite-sized pieces
- 1 cucumber, peeled, thinly sliced or cubed
- bell pepper, any variety, sliced or cubed
- cherry tomatoes
- black olives
- ½ cup Italian dressing
- 3 Tbs. Parmesan cheese

1 Cook pasta as directed on package. Rinse with cold water for 1 minute.

2 Add all the vegetables.

3 Toss with dressing. Sprinkle Parmesan cheese in last and toss gently.

Jell-O Salad

SERVINGS 8 • PREP TIME 10 minutes • COOK TIME 0 minutes

- 1 20 oz. can mixed fruit, drained
- 1 cup small curd cottage cheese
- 1 cup whipped cream
- 1 pkg. any flavor Jell-O® gelatin
- ½ cup chopped walnuts
- Cool Whip®

1 Combine all ingredients in mixing bowl. Blend in Jell-O® well with a spoon.

2 Place in serving dish and refrigerate until ready to serve.

3 Garnish with light scoop of Cool Whip® when serving.

Lemony Chicken Salad

SERVINGS 4 • PREP TIME 20 minutes • COOK TIME 10 minutes

- 3 cups coarsely grated celery
- 1 cup cooked chicken breast strips
- 2 Tbs. shredded ham

Sauce:

- ⅓ cup low-sodium, fat-free chicken broth
- 3 Tbs. fresh lemon juice
- 2 Tbs. light corn syrup
- 2 Tbs. rice vinegar
- 1 Tbs. grated lemon peel
- 3 garlic cloves, minced

1 Whisk sauce ingredients in small bowl.

2 Arrange the shredded celery on a serving plate.

3 Add a layer of chicken strips and top with a sprinkling of ham.

4 Spoon the sauce on the salad and serve.

Macaroni Salad

SERVINGS 8–10 • PREP TIME 15 minutes • COOK TIME 15 minutes

- 2 cups elbow macaroni
- block cheese
- ¾ cup mayonnaise
- 2 Tbs. yellow mustard
- ¼ cup sweet pickle relish
- ½ tsp. salt
- ¼ tsp. black pepper

1 Cook macaroni as directed on package. Rinse in cold water and place in lg. bowl.

2 Cut cheese block into bite-size pieces.

3 Combine cheese and remaining ingredients with the macaroni and toss well.

4 Chill until ready to serve.

Salads & Dressings

Oriental Chicken Salad

SERVINGS 12 • PREP TIME 20 minutes • COOK TIME 0 minutes

- 1 head of cabbage, finely chopped
- 1 10 oz. can chicken, drained
- 1 bunch green onions, finely chopped
- 2 bags Top Ramen noodles
- 1 cup sunflower seeds
- ½ cup slivered almonds

Dressing:
- ¾ cups vegetable oil
- 4 Tbs. sugar
- 6 Tbs. vinegar
- 2 seasoning packs from Top Ramen

1. Toss all dry ingredients together in lg. bowl.
2. In small bowl, combine dressing ingredients and whisk well.
3. Toss before serving. It's best to make the day before and refrigerate.

Pear & Walnut Spring Mix Salad

SERVINGS 6 • PREP TIME 20 minutes • COOK TIME 0 minutes

- 6 cups spring mix lettuce
- 1 Tbs. green onions, minced
- 2 Tbs. extra-virgin olive oil
- 2 tsp. white wine vinegar
- ¼ tsp. salt
- ¼ tsp. Dijon mustard
- ⅛ tsp. fresh ground black pepper
- 2 Bosc pears, thinly sliced
- ¼ cup chopped walnuts, toasted

1. Place lettuce in lg. bowl; whisk together the next 6 ingredients.
2. Gently toss dressing with salad.
3. Sprinkle walnuts over salad and arrange pears over the top.

Potato Salad

SERVINGS 8–10 • PREP TIME 20 minutes • COOK TIME 25 minutes

- 5 lbs. russet or red potatoes
- 8 hard boiled eggs
- 1 sm. yellow onion, chopped
- ¼ cup sweet pickle relish
- 2 Tbs. yellow mustard
- ¾ cup mayonnaise
- 1 tsp. salt
- ½ tsp. black pepper
- paprika

1 Peel potatoes and cube. Boil in lg. stock pot until tender.

2 In smaller pot, hard boil eggs.

3 Dice 6 eggs, thinly slice 2 eggs.

4 In lg. bowl, combine diced eggs with remaining ingredients (except paprika), and toss until well coated.

5 Place sliced eggs on top of finished salad. Sprinkle with paprika.

6 Chill until ready to serve. Adjust mayonnaise to the desired creaminess.

To hard boil eggs, place them in lg. stock pot and cover with water. Bring to full boil for 5 minutes. Turn off heat, leaving pot on hot burner. Cover pot and let sit for 15 minutes. Transfer eggs to bowl of ice water and let sit for 10 minutes. This process will help eggs to peel well.

To make 1 cup sour milk, combine 1½ to 2 Tbs. vinegar or lemon juice and enough milk to measure 1 cup. Let stand 5 minutes.

Salads & Dressings

Red Wine Vinaigrette Dressing

SERVINGS 1¼ cups • PREP TIME 5 minutes • COOK TIME 0 minutes

- ½ cup olive oil
- ½ cup red wine vinegar
- ½ cup sugar
- 2 tsp. Dijon mustard
- ¼ tsp. dried oregano
- ¼ tsp. black pepper

1 Place all ingredients in a salad dressing bottle and shake well. Refrigerate.

Summer Fruit Salad

SERVINGS 8 • PREP TIME 15 minutes • COOK TIME 0 minutes

- 1 20 oz. can pineapple chunks
- 1 11 oz. can mandarin oranges
- 2 Tbs. honey
- 2 Tbs. cornstarch
- 1 tsp. lemon juice
- 1 cantaloupe
- 2 bananas
- 2 cups seedless grapes
- ½ cup plain yogurt
- 1 cup mini marshmallows

1 Drain pineapple and mandarin oranges, reserving 1 cup of juice from either fruit or a combination of both.

2 Blend honey and cornstarch with reserved juice. Microwave on high 3 minutes or until mixture boils and thickens, stirring twice.

3 Stir in lemon juice and cool.

4 Cut cantaloupe and bananas into bite-sized pieces.

5 In lg. bowl, mix all fruit lightly.

6 Add thickened fruit juice to yogurt; gently mix into fruit until coated lightly.

7 Add marshmallows. Cover and refrigerate until chilled.

*Any fruit combination can be used as well as any flavor of yogurt.
*Add walnut pieces if desired.

Salads & Dressings

Summer Special Salad

SERVINGS 6 • PREP TIME 15 minutes • COOK TIME 0 minutes

- 1 lg. cauliflower, sliced
- 2 tomatoes, cut up
- 1 cucumber, sliced
- ½ cup radish, thinly sliced
- 6 green onions, chopped
- 1 green bell pepper, chopped
- ½ cup stuffed green olives, chopped
- ½ cup celery, chopped

Dressing:
- 1 cup Miracle Whip
- ¼ cup horseradish
- ¼ cup sugar
- 1 tsp. salt
- ¼ tsp. black pepper

1 Combine vegetables in a lg. salad bowl.

2 Whisk dressing ingredients and pour over vegetables. Can be made up in lg. amount and refrigerated for up to 2 weeks.

Thousand Island Dressing

SERVINGS 3 cups • PREP TIME 15 minutes • COOK TIME 0 minutes

- 1 pt. Miracle Whip
- ½ pt. mayonnaise
- 1 cup tomato soup
- 4 sweet pickles, grated
- 1 very sm. garlic bud, grated
- 1 sm. onion (size of an egg), grated

- 2 Tbs. vinegar
- 2 Tbs. sweet pickle juice
- 1 tsp. dry mustard
- 1 Tbs. chili sauce
- 1 Tbs. sugar

1 Combine all ingredients and whisk well or place in a shaker.

2 Store in jar in refrigerator for several weeks.

Tossed Salad with Walnuts and Cranberries

SERVINGS 8 • PREP TIME 15 minutes • COOK TIME 0 minutes

- 1 head of romaine lettuce
- 1 head of iceberg lettuce
- 1 cup broccoli spears
- 1 carrot
- 1 sm. tomato,
- ½ cucumber
- 1 cup walnuts
- 1 cup dried cranberries
- ½ cup feta cheese

1. Cut up lettuces and place in lg. serving bowl.
2. Cut up veggies into med. bite-sized pieces. Layer over lettuce as each is prepared.
3. Toss in walnuts and cranberries.
4. Toss in cheese just before serving.
5. Serve with Red Wine Vinaigrette Dressing. (See recipe on page 66)

Turkey Salad

SERVINGS 6 • PREP TIME 10 minutes • COOK TIME 15 minutes

- 4 cups chopped turkey breast
- 1 cup pineapple tidbits
- 1 cup seedless grapes
- 1 cup chopped apples
- 1 cup chopped walnuts (optional)
- 1½ cups mayonnaise

1. Toss all ingredients and serve over bed of lettuce.

Alternately, you can wrap in flour tortillas to make wraps.

Salads & Dressings

Soups & Stews

Beef Stew — 71

Chicken & Vegetable Soup — 71

Chicken Tortilla Soup — 72

Chili — 73

Corn Chowder Soup — 72

Cream of Broccoli Soup — 73

Cream of Potato Soup — 74

Crock of Steak — 75

Hamburger or Chicken Soup — 74

To mince: cut with kitchen scissors or sharp knife into very small pieces.

NOTES

Beef Stew

SERVINGS 4 • PREP TIME 20 minutes • COOK TIME 8 hours

- 1½ pounds beef tips
- ½ tsp. All Season Salt
- ¼ tsp. pepper
- ½ tsp. garlic powder
- 2 cups water
- 4 sm. white or red potatoes, cubed
- 1 sm. onion, chopped
- 2 celery sticks, chopped
- 1 can corn
- 1 sm. bag carrots
- 1 sm. bag peas
- 1 seasoning pack for beef stew

1. Coat beef tips with flour seasoned with All Season Salt, pepper, and garlic powder. Brown in hot oil, but do not fully cook.
2. Place in slow cooker. Add 2 cups water along with vegetables and seasoning pack.
3. Cook all day on high.

Chicken & Vegetable Soup

SERVINGS 6 • PREP TIME 20 minutes • COOK TIME 2 hours + 8 minutes

- 6 cups water
- 4 chicken breasts, cut into bite-sized pieces
- 3 chicken bouillon cubes
- ½ tsp. salt
- ¼ tsp. black pepper
- ⅓ cup onion, chopped
- 1 bay leaf
- 1 16 oz. can tomatoes, diced
- 1 16 oz. can cream style corn
- 2 sm. zucchini, thinly sliced
- 1½ cups uncooked noodles

1. Combine water, chicken, bouillon cubes, salt, pepper, onion, and bay leaf to lg. stock pot.
2. Bring to a full boil. Reduce heat and simmer for 2 hours.
3. Remove chicken and bay leaf. Add tomatoes and their juice, corn, and zucchini to pot.
4. Bring to boil, stir in noodles, reduce heat and simmer 8 minutes or until noodles are almost tender.
5. Add chicken back in, cover and simmer until noodles are tender.

Soups & Stews

Chicken Tortilla Soup

SERVINGS 4–6 • PREP TIME 20 minutes • COOK TIME 40 minutes

- 1 whole chicken
- 1 sm. white onion
- 2 Tbs. oil
- 3 tsp. chicken base
- 1 jar roasted red peppers
- ½ tsp. cumin
- ½ tsp. red chili
- 2 garlic cloves, minced
- 1 tsp. salt
- cilantro
- 1 can sweet corn, drained
- 1 can seasoned black beans
- flour tortillas
- shredded cheese (optional)
- sour cream (optional)

1. Prepare chicken by boiling in lg. pot. You can use a whole roasted store-bought chicken; this will give soup more flavor.
2. In lg. stock pot, sauté onion, oil, red peppers, cumin, red chili, garlic, and salt.
3. Add cilantro and simmer 15 minutes.
4. Dice cooked chicken and add to soup pot with corn, black beans, and 2 cups water. Bring to a boil, then reduce heat and simmer 20 minutes.
5. Strain chicken broth from pot chicken was cooked in and add this stock to the soup pot. Add any extra chicken removed from bones.
6. If the soup is too thin, thicken by whisking together ½ cup cornstarch and 1 cup water. Whisk this mixture into the soup.
7. Cut flour tortillas into long strips. Fry in hot oil and drain on paper towels. Serve with soup along with cheese and sour cream, if desired.

Corn Chowder Soup

SERVINGS 6 • PREP TIME 5 minutes • COOK TIME 15 minutes

- 1 can whole corn, undrained
- 1 can cream of mushroom soup
- 1 can New England clam chowder soup
- 1 can cream of potato soup
- 4 cups milk
- 2 tsp. butter

1. Heat all ingredients in lg. stock pot on low heat, being careful not to scorch soup.
2. Serve in bread bowls or with crackers.

Soups & Stews

Chili

SERVINGS 6 • PREP TIME 10 minutes • COOK TIME 1 hour

- 1½ lbs. ground beef
- ¼ cup diced onion
- 2 lg. cans of Ranch-style beans
- 1 lg. can chili beans
- 1 sm. can tomato sauce
- 4 Tbs. chili powder
- ½ tsp. cayenne pepper
- 2 tsp. red crushed pepper

1. Brown ground beef with onion and drain.
2. Put remaining ingredients in lg. pot. Heat to boiling.
3. Reduce heat to low; simmer 1 hour.

Cream of Broccoli Soup

SERVINGS 4 • PREP TIME 10 minutes • COOK TIME 20 minutes

- 2 cups milk
- 2 chicken bouillon cubes
- 1 onion, finely chopped
- 3 Tbs. flour
- 1½ cups water
- 16 oz. bag frozen broccoli
- 1 cup cheddar cheese soup

1. In lg. saucepan, combine milk, bouillon cubes, onion, and flour to make gravy texture.
2. Add water to make a gravy-like thickness.
3. Add broccoli and soup.
4. Heat through on med. heat to keep from scorching soup. Serve in bread bowls for fun!

Cream of Potato Soup

SERVINGS 4 • PREP TIME 20 minutes • COOK TIME 30 minutes

- ½ cup chopped onion
- 2 Tbs. butter
- 6 to 8 potatoes
- milk
- salt and pepper
- ¼ tsp. thyme
- ½ cup sour cream
- ½ cup shredded cheese
- bacon bits

1. In lg. pot, brown onion in butter until tender or clear.
2. Add potatoes and 4 cups water; bring to a boil. Simmer on med. heat until potatoes are tender.
3. Add salt, pepper, and thyme. Continue to simmer 10 minutes.
4. Just before serving, add sour cream and cheese. Top each bowl with bacon bits.
5. Serve in bread bowls if desired. (These can be found in a bakery.)

Hamburger or Chicken Soup

SERVINGS 6 • PREP TIME 20 minutes • COOK TIME 45 minutes

- 1½ lbs. ground beef
- ¼ cup chopped onions
- 1 can Veg-All (mixed veggies)
- 1 can cut green beans
- 1 can whole kernel corn
- 5 potatoes, peeled and cubed
- 2 beef bouillon cubes

1. In skillet, brown ground beef and onions. Drain.
2. In lg. stock pot, combine meat and onions with remaining ingredients, adding water to cover everything. Heat to a hard boil.
3. Reduce heat to med. and cover. Simmer for 30 minutes or until potatoes are soft.

Variation: Use 3 lg. chicken breasts, cooked and cubed, and chicken bouillon cubes instead of beef.

Crock of Steak

SERVINGS 6 • PREP TIME 20 minutes • COOK TIME 10 hours

- 1 cup flour
- 1 tsp. seasoning salt
- ½ tsp. garlic salt
- ¼ tsp. black pepper
- 1-2 lbs. of round steak
- 1 lg. can stewed tomatoes
- 1 can mushrooms
- 1-2 green bell peppers, sliced
- 1 cup chopped carrots
- ½ cup chopped celery
- 1 sm. onion, chopped
- 1 can French-style green beans undrained
- salt and pepper to taste
- 2-3 Tbs. soy sauce
- 2 cups hot, cooked rice

1. Combine flour, seasoning salt, garlic salt, and black pepper.
2. Cut meat into serving size pieces. Add to flour mixture to coat. Brown in hot oil on both sides and place in slow cooker.
3. Add other ingredients except rice.
4. Cook on low for 10-12 hours or on high for 4-5 hours.
5. Serve over hot rice.

Make a meal plan for two weeks. Shop for everything in one trip. This will help keep the cost down.

Soups & Stews

NOTES

Main Dishes

Baked Chicken	79
Baked Chicken Swiss	79
Chicken Bake with Wild Rice	80
Beef & Bean Green Chile Burritos	80
Cashew Chicken Stir Fry	81
Chicken Alfredo	82
Chicken and Biscuit Casserole	83
Chicken Enchiladas	84
Chicken Kiev	85
Chicken Pot Pie	86
Chicken with Pineapple	87
Chicken Stir Fry	88
Chicken Taco Casserole	89
Cornish Game Hens with Garlic & Rosemary	90
Cube Steaks with White Gravy	91
Deluxe Chicken Enchiladas	92
Italian Sausage and Vegetable Linguini	91
Lemon Teriyaki Glazed Chicken	83
Meatloaf	89
Non-Fried Fish & Chips with Slaw	93
Parmesan Chicken	94
Parmesan Pepper Steak	94
Pork Chop Casserole	95
Pork Chops with Cranberry Mustard Sauce	96
Pork Roast or Chops with Ginger Sauce	95
Pot Roast	97
Red Chile Enchiladas	98

Rice & Beef Hot Dish	98
Roasted Lemon Herb Chicken	99
Salisbury Steak	100
Sausage & Peppers with Bow Tie Pasta	99
Savory Pepper Steak	101
Sloppy Joes	101
Spaghetti with Meat Sauce	102
Succulent Baked Chicken	103
Teriyaki Chicken	103
Teriyaki Chicken Kabobs	104
Tuna & Biscuits with White Gravy	104

Plan your meals two weeks at a time before shopping. Several meals will use same ingredients—make the most of it.

Baked Chicken

SERVINGS 4 • PREP TIME 10 minutes • COOK TIME 30 minutes

- 4 boneless, skinless chicken breasts
- seasoning salt
- garlic salt
- black pepper
- thyme

1. Preheat oven to 375° F. In small bowl, combine all seasonings.
2. Cut chicken breasts in half lengthwise.
3. Spray chicken with cooking spray, flip pieces over and season, and spray other side.
4. Bake for 30 minutes until done, depending on thickness of chicken.

Baked Chicken Swiss

SERVINGS 4 • PREP TIME 10 minutes • COOK TIME 1 hour

- 3 chicken breasts, halved lengthwise
- 6 slices Swiss cheese
- 1 can cream of chicken soup
- ¼ cup dry white wine
- garlic-onion croutons
- ¼ cup butter, melted
- salt & pepper to taste
- rice or pasta for side

1. Preheat oven to 350° F. Spray 9" x 13" baking dish and place chicken in dish.
2. Cover each piece of chicken with slice of cheese.
3. Combine soup with wine and pour over chicken.
4. Crush enough croutons to cover top of chicken, and sprinkle over the chicken.
5. Drizzle with melted butter and add salt and pepper to taste. Bake uncovered for 1 hour.
6. Serve over rice or buttered pasta.

Main Dishes

Chicken Bake with Wild Rice

SERVINGS 4–6 • PREP TIME 10 minutes • COOK TIME 1½ hours

- ¾ cup wild rice
- ½ cup white rice
- 1 can beef consommé
- 2½ -3 lbs. chicken breasts or thighs
- 1 box dry onion soup mix (10 oz.)
- 1 can cream of mushroom soup
- 2 cups water

1. Preheat oven to 325° F. Combine wild and white rice in 9" x 13" pan.
2. Pour consommé over rice and stir. Spread evenly over bottom of pan.
3. Shake chicken in dry onion soup mix. Arrange on top of rice.
4. Combine mushroom soup with water and pour over chicken and rice.
5. Bake for 1 hour. Cover and bake for another 30 minutes.

Beef & Bean Green Chile Burritos

SERVINGS 6 • PREP TIME 10 minutes • COOK TIME 10 minutes

- 1 lb. ground beef
- 3 Tbs. onions, finely chopped
- 1 3 oz. can diced green chiles
- 1 20 oz. can refried beans
- 6 flour tortillas
- shredded cheese
- guacamole
- sour cream

1. In lg. skillet, brown ground beef with onions and green chiles. Drain.
2. Spoon refried beans into ground beef mixture and heat through.
3. Spoon mixture onto center of each tortilla; add cheese, guacamole, and sour cream as desired. Roll up.

*Fry in hot oil to make chimichangas.

Main Dishes

Cashew Chicken Stir Fry

SERVINGS 6 • PREP TIME 20 minutes • COOK TIME 15 minutes

- 2 cups chicken broth, divided
- 1 lb. boneless chicken breast, cut in ½ inch strips
- 2 garlic cloves, minced
- ½ cup thinly sliced carrots
- ½ cup celery, cut in ½ inch pieces
- 3 cups broccoli florets
- 1 cup fresh or frozen snow peas
- ¼ cup cornstarch
- 3 Tbs. soy sauce
- ½ tsp. ground ginger
- 1½ cups cashews
- hot cooked rice or low mein noodles

1 In a lg. skillet, heat 3 Tbs. broth. Add chicken and sauté in broth until no longer pink, about 3 to 5 minutes. Remove and keep warm.

2 Add garlic, carrots, and celery; stir fry for 3 minutes. Add broccoli and snow peas; stir fry for 4 to 5 minutes more.

3 Whisk together cornstarch, soy sauce, ginger, and remaining broth.

4 Stir broth mixture and chicken into skillet. Cook and stir until sauce thickens. Remove from heat and stir in cashews.

5 Serve over hot rice or low mein noodles.

Everyone in the family should have a job to do for each meal.

Main Dishes

Chicken Alfredo

SERVINGS 6 • PREP TIME 15 minutes • COOK TIME 45 minutes

- 2 eggs, beaten
- ½ cup milk
- 4 chicken breasts
- 1½ cups dry bread crumbs
- 2 Tbs. margarine
- 3 Tbs. flour

- 1½ c. milk
- 1 clove garlic
- ¼ tsp. white pepper
- ¼ tsp. ground nutmeg
- 8 oz. cooked fettuccine
- ¼ c. Parmesan cheese

1 Preheat oven to 375° F. Combine eggs and milk. Dip chicken in egg mixture and then in bread crumbs. Place on cookie sheet sprayed with cooking spray.

2 When all chicken is on the sheet, spray chicken with cooking spray.

3 Bake for 30 minutes or until chicken is done. Slice chicken into strips.

4 Melt butter in lg. skillet; whisk in flour. Whisk in milk; add seasonings. Cook over low to med. heat.

5 Cream sauce will thicken as it cooks. Simmer until chicken is ready. Add cooked fettuccine to sauce.

6 Place pasta on the plate and add 4 strips of chicken. Serve with green vegetables, toasted bread, and salad.

*Shrimp can be used instead of chicken. Prepare the same; lightly sauté the shrimp before placing on pasta.

Chicken and Biscuit Casserole

SERVINGS 4 • PREP TIME 10 minutes • COOK TIME 1 hours

- 2 cups chopped, cooked chicken
- 10 oz. cooked broccoli
- 1 10.5 oz. can cream of mushroom soup
- ¼ cup sour cream

Topping:
- ½ cup shredded cheddar cheese
- 10 wheat biscuits, halved horizontally
- 1 Tbs. roast seasoning
- ¼ cup sour cream
- 1 egg

1 Preheat oven to 375° F. In mixing bowl, combine chicken, broccoli, soup, and ¼ cup sour cream. Pour into greased 1½ qt. casserole dish.

2 Bake until hot and bubbly, about 20 to 25 minutes.

3 Remove from oven, sprinkle with cheese, and arrange biscuit halves on top.

4 Mix remaining ingredients and drizzle over biscuits.

5 Return casserole to oven and continue baking, uncovered, 25-30 minutes.

Lemon Teriyaki Glazed Chicken

SERVINGS 4-6 • PREP TIME 10 minutes • COOK TIME 35 minutes

- ½ cup lemon juice
- ½ cup soy sauce
- ¼ cup sugar
- 3 Tbs. brown sugar
- 2 Tbs. water
- 4 garlic cloves, minced
- ¾ tsp. ginger
- 8 chicken thighs
- cooked rice
- cooked snow peas and carrots

1 In skillet, combine all ingredients through ginger. Cook over med. heat for 3 to 4 minutes.

2 Add chicken and cover. Simmer 30 minutes or until done.

3 Serve over rice with snow peas and carrots. Spoon extra sauce over chicken.

Main Dishes

Chicken Enchiladas

SERVINGS 6 • PREP TIME 15 minutes • COOK TIME 35 minutes

- 1 lg. can cream of mushroom soup
- 1 sm. can diced green chiles
- 1 cup sour cream
- 4 chicken breasts, boiled and cubed
- 6 flour tortillas
- 2 cups shredded cheese

1. Preheat oven to 375° F. Combine soup and green chiles in med. saucepan; heat until hot and bubbly. Turn heat off, stir in sour cream. Set aside.
2. Spoon some of the soup mixture onto the bottom of a 9" x 13" pan.
3. Place some chicken cubes down middle of a tortilla, spoon soup mixture over chicken, and sprinkle cheese on top.
4. Roll up by bringing two sides half way up, then turn to roll up lengthwise. Place each tortilla on top of soup in prepared pan.
5. Pour remaining soup mixture over enchiladas. Add water to soup mixture, if needed.
6. Bake for 25 minutes. Remove from oven, sprinkle with cheese, return to oven for 10 minutes or until cheese is melted.

Chicken Kiev

SERVINGS 4 • PREP TIME 10 minutes • COOK TIME 30 minutes

- 4 boneless chicken breasts
- 4 Tbs. softened butter
- 4 oz. Monterey Jack cheese, cut into 8 strips
- 5 Tbs. melted butter
- 1 cup seasoned bread crumbs
- 8 toothpicks
- rice, cooked as directed

1. Gently pound breasts between waxed paper with flat kitchen mallet to ¼" thick. Cut each breast in half.

2. Spread ½ Tbs. softened butter across each piece and lay a strip of cheese over butter.

3. Fold lower edge of chicken over cheese and roll up. Secure with toothpick.

4. Dip each bundle in melted butter and drain briefly; roll in breadcrumbs until evenly coated.

5. Place bundles seam-side down on a 9" x 13" pan. Drizzle any remaining butter over chicken.

6. Cover and refrigerate at least 4 hours or overnight.

7. Bake at 450° F. for 30 minutes or until hot. Serve over hot rice.

Chicken Pot Pie

SERVINGS 6 • PREP TIME 15 minutes • COOK TIME 30 to 40 minutes

- ½ cup butter
- ⅓ cup flour
- 1 cup milk
- 1 can chicken broth
- ½ tsp. salt
- ¼ tsp. pepper
- 3 chicken bouillon cubes
- ½ tsp. thyme
- 6 boneless chicken breasts, cooked and cubed
- 2 cups frozen mixed veggies, thawed
- 2 boxes ready pie crust

1. Prehead oven to 400° F. Melt butter in lg. saucepan. Whisk in flour; mixture will be thick. Slowly whisk in milk.

2. Stir in chicken broth, salt, pepper, bouillon, and thyme. Cook until thickened.

3. Add chicken and vegetables. Heat through.

4. Line a pie pan with a pie crust. Pour in the chicken mixture. Top with remaining pie crust. Cut a couple of slits in top crust.

5. Bake for 30 to 40 minutes, until golden brown.

This can be made in single serving dishes by cutting pie crust to fit. Baking time will vary depending on size of dish.

Treat your family like guests and your guests like family.

Chicken with Pineapple

SERVINGS 8 • PREP TIME 20 minutes • COOK TIME 30 minutes

- 20 oz. can pineapple chunks
- 1 Tbs. olive oil
- 8 chicken breasts, cut in 1/2" slices
- 2 garlic cloves, minced fine
- 1 red bell pepper, cut into chucks
- 1 green bell pepper, cut into chunks
- 1 small yellow onion, cut into chunks
- 1 Tbs. fresh ginger, minced
- 1 Tbs. cornstarch
- 1½ cups snow peas
- ½ cup chicken broth
- 2 Tbs. light soy sauce
- 1 Tbs. hoisin sauce
- ¼ tsp. ground cinnamon
- 2 Tbs. honey
- 2 cups cooked white rice

1. Drain pineapple and save juice.
2. Heat oil in lg. skillet. Cook chicken until no longer pink, about 5 minutes.
3. Add garlic, peppers, onion, and ginger and sauté for about 3 minutes.
4. Whisk ¼ cup of reserved pineapple juice with cornstarch, set aside.
5. Add snow peas, remaining pineapple juice, soy sauce, hoisin sauce, cinnamon, and honey to skillet. Cook 5 minutes.
6. Add pineapple chunks and juice-cornstarch mixture; cook until thickened, about 3 minutes.

Serve over hot rice.

Main Dishes

Chicken Stir Fry

SERVINGS 6 • PREP TIME 20 minutes • COOK TIME 15 minutes

- 2 Tbs. soy sauce
- ¼ tsp. ginger
- 1 lg. chicken, cooked, deboned, cut into bite sized pieces
- oil for sautéing
- carrots
- celery
- onion
- bell pepper
- broccoli
- snow peas
- 2 Tbs. cornstarch
- 1 cup water
- 1 chicken bouillon cube
- cooked rice

1. Whisk together soy sauce, garlic and ginger. Pour over chicken and let sit at room temperature while preparing veggies.
2. Cut up all vegetables and set aside.
3. Sauté chicken in hot oil until no longer pink. Remove from skillet and set aside, leaving liquid in skillet.
4. In same skillet, add vegetables to oil. Cook until almost tender. Add chicken with vegetables and heat through.
5. Prepare sauce by whisking together; pour over chicken and vegetables.
6. Cook on med. heat until sauce thickens. Serve over hot rice.

Brown a large package of ground beef at one time and divide into freezer bags for optional dinners. Be sure to date each bag.

Main Dishes

Chicken Taco Casserole

SERVINGS 4 • PREP TIME 20 minutes • COOK TIME 1 hour

- 1 lg. onion, diced
- 1 Tbs. butter
- 1 can cream of mushroom soup
- 1 can cream of chicken soup
- 1 can chicken broth
- 8 oz. mild or hot salsa
- 1 pkg. corn tortillas
- 4 chicken breasts, boiled and diced
- shredded cheese
- corn chips

1 Preheat oven to 350° F. Sauté chopped onion in butter. Add in soups, broth, and salsa. Heat through.

2 Layer in oven safe casserole dish in order given:
  – sauce
  – corn tortillas
  – chicken
  – cheese
Repeat for 2 layers; on third layer do not add cheese.

3 Bake for 45 minutes. Remove from oven and add cheese on top of casserole.

4 Return to oven for additional 15 minutes or until cheese has melted.

5 Serve with corn chips.

Meatloaf

SERVINGS 6 • PREP TIME 15 minutes • COOK TIME 1 hour 15 minutes

- 2 lbs. ground beef
- ¼ cup onions, chopped fine
- 2 Tbs. chopped green bell peppers
- 1 8 oz. can tomato sauce
- ½ sleeve of crackers, crushed fine
- 1 Tbs. seasoning salt
- ½ tsp. garlic salt
- 1 cup ketchup
- ¼ cup brown sugar

1 Preheat oven to 375° F. Mix all ingredients except ketchup and brown sugar. Press into meatloaf pan.

2 Bake for 1 hour. Remove from oven and drain off fat.

3 Combine ketchup and brown sugar; spread over top and bake another 15 minutes.

Main Dishes

Cornish Game Hens with Garlic & Rosemary

SERVINGS 4 • PREP TIME 15 minutes • COOK TIME 50 minutes

- 4 Cornish game hens
- 3 Tbs. olive oil
- salt and pepper
- 1 lemon, quartered
- 4 sprigs fresh rosemary

- 24 gloves garlic
- ⅓ cup white wine
- ⅓ cup low-sodium chicken broth
- 4 sprigs fresh rosemary for garnish

1. Preheat oven to 450° F. Rub hens with 1 Tbs. of the oil. Lightly season hens with salt and pepper.
2. Place 1 lemon wedge and 1 sprig of rosemary in cavity of each hen.
3. Arrange in lg. roasting pan and arrange garlic cloves around hens. Roast in preheated oven for 25 minutes.
4. Reduce oven temperature to 350° F.
5. In a mixing bowl, whisk together wine, chicken broth, and remaining 2 Tbs. of oil; pour over hens.
6. Continue to roast about 25 minutes longer. Hens should be golden brown and juices should run clear.
7. Baste with pan juice every 10 minutes during last 30 minutes or roasting.
8. Transfer hens to serving platter, pouring any cavity juice into roasting pan as you do. Tent foil over the hens to keep warm.
9. In a med. saucepan, combine juices from roasting pan with garlic cloves and boil until liquids reduce to a sauce consistency, about 5 minutes.
10. Cut hens lengthwise to serve and serve sauce on the side.

Cube Steaks with White Gravy

SERVINGS 6 • PREP TIME 15 minutes • COOK TIME 35 minutes

- 2 cups flour
- 1 tsp. seasoning salt
- ¼ tsp. garlic salt
- ⅛ tsp. black pepper
- 6 cube steaks, cut in half
- 3 Tbs. oil
- 1 lg. can cream of mushroom soup
- 2 cups milk

1 In med. bowl, combine flour, seasoning salt, garlic salt, and black pepper. Coat each piece of cube steak in flour mixture.

2 In lg. skillet, heat oil and then add meat. You may need to cook 4 at a time, depending on the size of your skillet, browning both sides.

3 Whisk together the soup and milk. Pour over meat and bring to boil. Reduce heat and simmer for 25 minutes.

Serve with mashed potatoes and vegetables.

Italian Sausage and Vegetable Linguini

SERVINGS 4 • PREP TIME 15 minutes • COOK TIME 20 minutes

- 1 8 oz. pkg. linguini
- 1 lb. Italian sausage, sliced
- 2 Tbs. olive oil
- 5 green and red bell peppers, sliced into strips
- 1 sm. bag frozen peas
- 4 lg. carrots, peeled and sliced
- 3 oz. black olives
- 1 cup zesty Italian dressing
- garlic and oregano to taste

1 Cook pasta as directed on package.

2 Spray lg. skillet with cooking spray. When skillet is hot, sauté sausage until lightly brown.

3 Remove sausage, add olive oil, and sauté vegetables for 2 to 3 minutes.

4 Add pasta, olives, dressing, garlic, and oregano to taste. Simmer until hot. Serve warm.

Main Dishes

Deluxe Chicken Enchiladas

SERVINGS 6 • PREP TIME 15 minutes • COOK TIME 50 minutes

- 2 whole chicken breasts
- water
- 1 onion, diced
- 1 bay leaf
- dash of salt
- 1 Tbs. peppercorns
- 1 med. onion, chopped
- 3 Tbs. Parmesan cheese
- 8 oz. Monterey Jack cheese, shredded
- 1 4 oz. can green chiles
- 1 15 oz. can tomatillos, drained
- ¼ cup fresh cilantro leaves or 2 Tbs. dried
- ¾ cup whipping cream
- 1 egg
- 1 pkg. corn tortillas

1 Boil chicken with ½ of onion, bay leaf, salt and peppercorns. Shred chicken when it is done.

2 Combine remaining ½ of onion with cheeses; stir into shredded chicken and set aside.

3 Blend green chiles, cilantro, tomatillos, cream, and egg in blender.

4 Fry tortillas until limp. Add chicken mixture, roll up, place in baking dish, and pour sauce over all of it.

5 Bake at 375° F. for 20 minutes. Top with extra cheese and return to oven until cheese is melted.

6 Serve with sour cream, black olives, salsa, chopped tomatoes, and shredded lettuce.

To baste is to moisten foods during cooking time with pan drippings or sauce.

Non-Fried Fish & Chips with Slaw

SERVINGS 4 • PREP TIME 20 minutes • COOK TIME 35 minutes

Chips:

1. Scrub 2 lg. baking potatoes and cut in ½ inch wedges.

2. Position racks in oven in thirds. Heat to 500° F. degrees. Coat two jelly roll pans with cooking spray. Spread potatoes in one of the prepared pans.

3. Spray potatoes with cooking spray, toss to coat. Spread into single layer. Bake on lower oven rack 25 minutes, turning potatoes once, or until tender and golden. Sprinkle with salt while hot.

Fish:
- 2 Tbs. all-purpose flour
- ½ cup packaged seasoned bread crumbs
- 1 egg white, slightly beaten
- 4 flounder fillets, about 6 ounces each

1. Spread flour and bread crumbs on two separate pieces of waxed paper. Place egg white in shallow bowl. Coat fish with flour first, dip in egg white, then press in crumbs until coated.

2. Spray top of fillets with cooking spray. Place sprayed side down on other prepared pan. Spray top of fish.

3. Place on top oven rack 15 minutes after putting potatoes in oven.

4. Bake 7 to 10 minutes until crust is golden and fish is not shining in the middle when pierced with a knife.

Slaw:
- 4 cups shredded red or green cabbage
- 1 cup shredded carrots
- ½ cup scallions
- ½ cup bottled fat-free ranch dressing
- 1 Tbs. white cider vinegar
- ½ tsp. black pepper

1. Toss all together until well mixed. Serve with fish 'n' chips.

*Slaw can be made ahead of time.

Main Dishes

Parmesan Chicken

SERVINGS 6 • PREP TIME 15 minutes • COOK TIME 45 minutes

- 2 Tbs. butter
- ½ cup club crackers, crushed
- ¼ cup grated Parmesan cheese
- 1 tsp. onion powder
- ½ Tbs. dried parsley flakes
- ¼ tsp. garlic powder
- ⅛ tsp. black pepper
- 6 to 8 pieces of chicken, skinned

1 Preheat oven to 350° F. Melt butter and spread in bottom of 9" x 13" baking pan.

2 Combine cracker crumbs, cheese, seasonings, and herbs in bowl.

3 Coat chicken pieces in melted butter, then in crumb mixture and place in baking dish.

4 Sprinkle with remaining crumbs. Bake for 45 minutes.

Parmesan Pepper Steak

SERVINGS 4 • PREP TIME 15 minutes • COOK TIME 1 hour

- 1½ lbs. round steak cut in thin strips
- 2 Tbs. butter
- ½ cup French fried onions
- ½ cup green bell pepper, cut into chunks
- 1 clove garlic, minced
- 1 8 oz. can tomato sauce
- ¼ cup beef broth
- ¼ tsp. black pepper
- ¼ cup Parmesan cheese
- 2 Tbs. fresh parsley, chopped
- rice or egg noodles, cooked as directed on package

1 Brown meat in oil in lg. skillet for 2 minutes per side.

2 Add onions, peppers, and garlic; cook and stir in tomato sauce, beef broth, and black pepper. Bring to a boil.

3 Reduce heat; cover. Simmer 1 hour or until meat is tender, stirring occasionally.

4 Sprinkle with Parmesan cheese before serving. Serve over hot noodles or rice.

Pork Chop Casserole

SERVINGS 6 • PREP TIME 10 minutes • COOK TIME 1½ hours

- 6 pork chops
- oil
- 1 cup rice
- 1 sm. onion, thinly sliced
- 1 green bell pepper, thinly sliced
- 1 tomato, thinly sliced
- 3 cans beef consommé

1 Preheat oven to 325° F. Brown pork chops in hot oil on both sides until lightly browned.

2 Spread rice on bottom of dish; place pork chops on top of rice.

3 Lay vegetables on top of chops; sprinkle with salt and pepper.

4 Pour beef consommé over all and cover with foil.

5 Bake for 1½ hours.

Pork Roast or Chops with Ginger Sauce

SERVINGS 6 • PREP TIME 10 minutes • COOK TIME 2 hours

- 1½ lbs. pork roast or 6 pork chops
- 1 can cranberry sauce
- ¼ cup onion, finely chopped
- ¾ cup orange juice
- ¼ tsp. ginger
- ¼ tsp. ground cinnamon

1 Bake pork roast in roasting pan at 325° F. for 1 hour.

2 Combine all other ingredients and pour over roast, basting every 15 minutes during 1 more hour of baking.

3 Serve remaining juice from basting on the side.

Main Dishes

Pork Chops with Cranberry Mustard Sauce

SERVINGS 4 • PREP TIME 15 minutes • COOK TIME 30 minutes

- 4 pork chops with bones
- 1 12 oz. pkg. cranberries, fresh or frozen
- 1 cup water
- 1 cup sugar
- ½ cup chopped pecans or walnuts
- 4 tsp. Dijon mustard
- ½ cup cranberry sauce
- 4 tsp. Dijon mustard

1 Place pork chops in shallow baking dish. Wash cranberries and set aside.

2 In med. saucepan, add water and sugar; bring to a boil, stirring until sugar dissolves. Add cranberries and bring to boil again.

3 Reduce heat and simmer 10 minutes. Stir in nuts and mustard. Let cool completely to room temperature.

4 Brush mustard mixture over both sides of chops and refrigerate about 1 hour to marinate.

5 Spray lg. nonstick frying pan with cooking spray; when pan is hot, add chops and cook 10 minutes, partially covered.

6 Uncover pan and turn chops. Cook, uncovered, about 5 to 10 minutes.

7 Pour sauce over chops or serve on the side.

Pot Roast

SERVINGS 6 • PREP TIME 20 minutes • COOK TIME 4 hours

- 4 to 5 lbs. beef pot roast
- ½ cup flour
- ½ tsp. paprika
- ¼ tsp. black pepper
- 1 tsp. seasoning salt
- ½ tsp. garlic salt
- 2 Tbs. oil
- 1 cup water or red wine
- 1 lg. onion, quartered
- 10 med. carrots
- 10 celery stalks
- 10 med. potatoes, peeled and quartered
- 1 tsp. salt
- 2 Tbs. minced fresh parsley
- 2 Tbs. flour
- ¼ cup water

1. Preheat oven to 300° F. Mix flour, paprika, black pepper, seasoning salt, and garlic salt; rub into roast. Brown in hot oil in lg. skillet on both sides. Add water.

2. Place in lg. roaster. Cover and bake for 3 hours.

3. Add vegetables and continue baking for another 45 minutes or until vegetables are tender. Transfer meat to serving platter.

4. To make gravy, pour drippings from pan into small saucepan. Whisk in flour and water gradually; continue stirring until it boils. Boil 1 minute.

Red Chili Enchiladas

SERVINGS 6 • PREP TIME 15 minutes • COOK TIME 20 minutes

- 1½ lbs. ground beef
- 1 sm. onion, chopped
- ½ cup flour
- 1 lg. can tomato juice
- ½ Tbs. red chili powder
- 1 tsp. oregano
- ½ tsp. cumin
- garlic salt to taste
- 6 lg. flour tortillas
- 2 cups shredded cheese
- sour cream
- salsa

1 Brown ground beef and onion. Add flour to absorb fat for thickening.

2 Add tomato juice, chili powder, oregano, cumin, and garlic salt. Simmer 20 minutes or until flavors blend.

3 Place lg. spoonful of meat mixture onto flour tortilla, adding cheddar cheese, sour cream, or salsa to your liking. Roll up and serve warm.

Rice & Beef Hot Dish

SERVINGS 4 • PREP TIME 10 minutes • COOK TIME 1½ hours

- 1 lb. ground beef browned with onion, drained
- 1 cup celery
- ½ cup rice
- 1 can cream of mushroom soup
- 1 can cream of chicken soup
- 2 cups water
- 2 Tbs. soy sauce

1 Preheat oven to 350° F. Combine all ingredients in 9" x 13" baking dish.

2 Bake for 1½ hours.

3 Stir after first 30 minutes.

Main Dishes

Roasted Lemon Herb Chicken

SERVINGS 4 • PREP TIME 10 minutes • COOK TIME 1½ hours

- 2 Tbs. Italian seasoning
- ½ tsp. seasoning salt
- ½ tsp. mustard powder
- 1 tsp. garlic powder
- ½ tsp. ground black pepper
- 4 chicken breasts
- 2 lemons
- 2 Tbs. olive oil

1. Preheat oven to 350° F. Combine Italian seasoning, seasoning salt, mustard powder, garlic powder, and pepper and set aside.

2. Place chicken in 9" x 13" baking dish. Rub chicken with the seasonings.

3. In small bowl, whisk the juice of the lemons and olive oil. Drizzle over chicken.

4. Bake for 1½ hours, basting every 30 minutes with juices in pan.

Sausage & Peppers with Bow Tie Pasta

SERVINGS 4 • PREP TIME 20 minutes • COOK TIME 20 minutes

- 4 cups bow tie pasta, cooked
- 12 oz. Italian sausage
- 2 med. red bell peppers
- ¼ sm. onion
- ½ cup carrots
- ½ cup broth, beef or vegetable
- ¼ tsp. black pepper
- ¼ cup fresh parsley

1. Cut sausage at an angle into ¼ inch strips. Cut pepper, onions, and carrots into thin strips.

2. Sauté sausage with veggies. Add broth into skillet and bring to boil. Reduce heat and simmer 5 minutes.

3. Remove from heat and pour over pasta. Add parsley to top. Stir gently. Serve with garlic bread and salad.

Main Dishes

Salisbury Steak

SERVINGS 6 • PREP TIME 20 minutes • COOK TIME 1 hour

- 1 sm. onion, finely chopped
- 1 green bell pepper, finely chopped
- 2 Tbs. oil
- ¾ cup bread crumbs *
- 3 Tbs. milk
- 4 eggs
- 1 tsp. salt
- ½ tsp. black pepper
- ½ tsp. garlic powder
- 3 tsp. Worcestershire sauce
- ¾ tsp. cumin
- 2 lbs. lean ground beef
- 2 brown gravy packets

1 Preheat oven to 375° F. Sauté onion and bell pepper in hot oil just until tender.

2 Combine vegetables with remaining ingredients in order given, except gravy mix. Blend well with hands or in a mixer.

3 Shape into balls the size of your palm. Press into ½ inch patties and shape into oblong shape.

4 Grill each patty about 3 minutes on the grill or in a skillet on the stove top.

5 Cascade patties into a 9" x 13" pan. Make gravy mix as directed on pkg. and pour over meat patties.

6 Bake for 45 minutes.

*Bread crumbs can be made from dried bread, saltine crackers, or croutons.

Have another family over for dinner and have them bring half the meal.

Main Dishes

Savory Pepper Steak

SERVINGS 4 • PREP TIME 15 minutes • COOK TIME 15 minutes

- 1 lb. stir fry beef strips or sirloin, thinly sliced
- ½ green, red and yellow peppers, thinly sliced
- 1 med. onion, thinly sliced
- 3 beef bouillon cubes
- ½ cup water
- 3 cups cooked rice

1 Spray lg. non-stick skillet with cooking spray. Brown meat over med. high heat until tender and brown.

2 Add peppers, onion, bouillon cubes, and ½ cup water. Cook until vegetables are tender-crispy.

3 Serve over hot rice.

Sloppy Joes

SERVINGS 6 • PREP TIME 5 minutes • COOK TIME 20 minutes

- 1 lb. ground beef
- 2 Tbs. onions, finely chopped
- 1 can chicken gumbo soup
- 3 Tbs. ketchup
- 1 Tbs. mustard
- 1 pkg. hamburger buns

1 Cook ground beef and onion in lg. skillet.

2 Add soup, ketchup, and mustard; bring to a boil.

3 Turn heat down to med. low and simmer 15 minutes.

4 Serve on toasted buns.

Main Dishes

Spaghetti with Meat Sauce

SERVINGS vary • PREP TIME 15 minutes • COOK TIME 3 hours

- 1 6½ lb. can or 6–29 oz. cans tomato sauce
- 1 20 oz. can tomato paste
- ¼ cup Italian seasoning
- 2 garlic cloves, minced
- 2 Tbs. oregano flakes
- 2 Tbs. parsley flakes
- 2 tsp. black pepper
- 2 tsp. salt

1 Combine all ingredients and simmer 2 to 3 hours. Sauce can be frozen in serving size portions in gallon size freezer bags.

2 For meat sauce, brown 1 lb. ground beef with 1 lb. Italian sausage. Combine with sauce and simmer 15 minutes. Pour over cooked spaghetti noodles.

*Whole grain pasta is good to use.

Pizza variations that are great for kid parties!

#1. Open 1 can of biscuits and pull apart to make 20. Place on cookie sheet, cover with spaghetti sauce mix, place two pepperonis and cheese on top. Bake at 400° F. for 15 minutes.

#2. Use sub sandwich bread, cut in half lengthwise. Put sauce, pepperoni, and cheese on top. Bake 400° F. for 20 minutes.

#3. Buy cheese ravioli in freezer section of the store. Prepare as directed on package. Rinse, pour some of the spaghetti sauce over the top and sprinkle with mozzarella cheese. Bake at 375° F. for 20 minutes.

Succulent Baked Chicken

SERVINGS 6 • PREP TIME 10 minutes • COOK TIME 45 minutes

- 1 cube sweet (unsalted) butter
- 1 Tbs. lemon juice
- 1 cup club crackers, finely crushed
- ½ tsp. garlic salt
- ½ tsp. black pepper
- 6 boneless chicken breasts

1 Preheat oven to 350° F. Melt butter, stir in lemon juice, set aside.

2 Mix cracker crumbs with garlic salt and pepper in med. bowl.

3 Dip chicken into butter/lemon mixture, roll in cracker crumbs, lay in baking dish sprayed with cooking spray. Sprinkle remaining crumbs on top of chicken.

4 Bake 30 minutes. Remove from oven, pour remaining butter/lemon mixture over the chicken and return to oven for 15 minutes.

Teriyaki Chicken

SERVINGS 4 • PREP TIME 5 minutes • COOK TIME 35 minutes

- ½ cup soy sauce
- ½ cup sugar
- 1½ tsp. red wine vinegar
- 2 tsp. oil
- 2 garlic cloves, minced
- ¼ tsp. ginger
- 1 lb. boneless chicken breast
- 1 cup rice, cooked as directed

1 Preheat oven to 350° F. Mix soy sauce, sugar, vinegar, oil, garlic, and ginger to make marinade.

2 Place chicken in marinade in baking dish. Bake for 35 minutes.

3 Serve over hot rice.

Teriyaki Chicken Kabobs

SERVINGS 4 • PREP TIME 20 minutes • COOK TIME 15 minutes

- ½ cup soy sauce
- ½ cup sugar
- 1½ tsp. red wine vinegar
- 2 tsp. oil
- 2 garlic cloves, minced
- ½ tsp. ginger
- 1 lb. boneless chicken breast
- 1 med. onion, chopped in lg. chunks
- 1 can pineapple chunks
- 2 cups cooked rice

1. Mix soy sauce, sugar, vinegar, oil, garlic, and ginger to make marinade.
2. Cut chicken into lg. bite sized pieces. Place chicken on skewers with onions and pineapple chunks.
3. Place chicken and marinade in dish and marinate for 1 hour.
4. Grill kabobs for 10 to 15 minutes, turning often. Serve over hot rice.

Use cooling racks on grill sprayed with cooking spray for place kabobs so they do not fall into the fire.

Tuna & Biscuits with White Gravy

SERVINGS 4 • PREP TIME 5 minutes • COOK TIME 15 minutes

- 1 can large biscuits
- 3 Tbs. butter
- ½ cup flour
- 1½ cups milk
- salt and pepper
- 2 cans tuna, drained

1. Bake biscuits as directed on can.
2. In lg. nonstick skillet, melt butter; stir in flour until crumbly. Stir in milk, salt, and pepper slowly. Bring to boil over med. heat.
3. The gravy will thicken as it cooks. Once gravy is thick, add tuna and heat through.
4. Pour tuna mixture over hot, buttered biscuits.

Main Dishes

Side Dishes

Baby Glazed Carrots	107
Baked Asparagus with Parmesan	107
Baked Beans	108
Baked Stuffed Zucchini	108
Baked Sweet Potatoes	109
Black Beans	109
Broccoli Casserole	110
Candied Yams	110
Corn Casserole	111
Country Baked Beans	111
Crunchy Potato Bake	112
Easy Potato Casserole	112
Green Bean Casserole	113
Green Bean Melody	113
Homemade French Fries	114
Mashed Sweet Potatoes	114
Mexican Coleslaw	115
Old Fashioned Scalloped Potatoes	115
Oven Baked Fried Potatoes	116
Oven Roasted Potatoes	116
Party Potatoes	117
Red Potatoes Baked or Grilled	117
Red Beans & Rice	118
Spanish Rice	118
Spinach Soufflé	119
Twice Baked Potatoes	120
Wagon Wheel Pasta with Salsa-Marinated Beans	121

NOTES

Baby Glazed Carrots

SERVINGS 4 • PREP TIME 5 minutes • COOK TIME 20 minutes

- 2 cups baby carrots
- ½ cup brown sugar
- ¼ cup butter

1 In med. saucepan, cook carrots in enough water to cover them. Boil until almost tender.

2 Drain most of water. Place back on stove and add butter and sugar.

3 Simmer on low to med. heat until carrots are tender.

Baked Asparagus with Parmesan

SERVINGS 4 • PREP TIME 5 minutes • COOK TIME 15 minutes

- 1 lg. bundle fresh asparagus
- olive oil
- Parmesan cheese
- dash of thyme and dill
- salt and pepper

1 Preheat oven to 350° F. Snap ends off asparagus and discard.

2 Place asparagus on cookie sheet. Drizzle oil over them and roll to coat.

3 Sprinkle seasonings on top of them. Sprinkle with cheese. Bake for 15 minutes.

Baked Beans

SERVINGS 4 • PREP TIME 5 minutes • COOK TIME 30 minutes

- 1 lg. can pork and beans
- ½ cup brown sugar
- 3 hot dogs, sliced
- ¼ cup onion finely diced
- ½ cup barbecue sauce

1 Preheat oven to 375° F. Combine all ingredients in oven-safe dish.

2 Bake for 30 minutes.

Baked Stuffed Zucchini

SERVINGS 6 • PREP TIME 10 minutes • COOK TIME 35 minutes

- 6 med. size zucchini
- 3 cups bread crumbs
- ½ cup grated Parmesan cheese
- ¼ cup onions, finely chopped
- 3 Tbs. parsley flakes
- ⅛ tsp. black pepper
- 1 tsp. salt
- 2 beaten eggs
- 2 Tbs. butter

1 Preheat oven to 350° F. Wash zucchini and cut off ends. Cook in lg. stock pot of boiling water for 5 minutes.

2 Remove from water and cut lengthwise; place in baking dish. Spoon out pulp and place in mixing bowl.

3 Combine bread crumbs, cheese, onion, parsley, black pepper, salt, and eggs. Mix with spoon to blend.

4 Fill each zucchini shell with filling and dot with butter. Sprinkle a little Parmesan cheese on top of each zucchini. Bake for 30 minutes.

Baked Sweet Potatoes

SERVINGS 4 • PREP TIME 5 minutes • COOK TIME 1 hour

- 4 lg. yams
- ¼ cup butter
- ¼ cup brown sugar
- Dash of ground cinnamon

1 Preheat oven to 400° F. Wash potatoes and wrap tightly in foil. Bake for 1 hour. Potatoes will be done when you can squeeze them and they feel soft.

2 Remove from foil and cut lengthwise. Add butter and sugar to each potato and sprinkle with cinnamon.

Black Beans

SERVINGS 4 • PREP TIME 10 minutes • COOK TIME 20 minutes

- 2 tsp. extra virgin olive oil
- 1 med. onion, diced
- 2 cloves garlic, minced
- 2 tsp. ground chile, ancho, or pasilla pepper
- ½ tsp. cumin,
- ½ tsp. dried oregano
- 30 oz. canned black beans
- 1 cup water
- 1 Tbs. tomato paste

1 Heat oil in a med. saucepan over med.-high heat. Add onion and cook, stirring, until translucent, 4 to 5 minutes.

2 Add garlic and cook, stirring constantly, for 30 seconds. Add ground pepper, cumin, and oregano. Cook, stirring, until fragrant, about 30 seconds more.

3 Add beans, 1 cup of water, and tomato paste; stir to combine.

4 Bring to a simmer, reduce heat to med.-low and cook, stirring occasionally, until the beans are heated through and the sauce is slightly thickened, 8 to 10 minutes. Serve warm.

To make ahead: Cover and refrigerate for up to 2 days. Reheat in a saucepan with 2 Tbs. water over med. low heat, stirring occasionally, for about 5 minutes.

Side Dishes

Broccoli Casserole

SERVINGS 4 • PREP TIME 15 minutes • COOK TIME 25 minutes

- 2 cups chopped broccoli spears
- 8 oz. Velveeta cheese
- ½ cup butter
- 40 Ritz crackers, finely crushed

1. Preheat oven to 350° F. Cook broccoli in boiling water for 3 minutes. Drain; reserve ¼ cup liquid.
2. Place broccoli and liquid into 9" x 13" pan.
3. Cube cheese and add over broccoli.
4. Melt ¼ cup butter and pour over broccoli.
5. Add other ¼ cup of butter to crushed crackers. Spread crackers over broccoli.
6. Bake 25 minutes.

Candied Yams

SERVINGS 4 • PREP TIME 5 minutes • COOK TIME 40 minutes

- 1 lg. can yams
- ½ cup brown sugar
- ½ tsp. ground cinnamon
- ¼ cup butter
- Mini marshmallows

1. Preheat oven to 350° F. Drain yams and place in casserole dish. Stir in sugar and cinnamon. Dot with butter.
2. Bake for 30 minutes.
3. Remove from oven; stir lightly to coat well.
4. Spread marshmallows over the top. Return to oven for 10 minutes more.

Side Dishes

Corn Casserole

SERVINGS 4 • PREP TIME 10 minutes • COOK TIME 45 minutes

- 8 oz. cream cheese
- ½ cup butter
- ½ cup milk
- 16 oz. frozen corn
- ¼ cup diced red bell pepper
- ¼ cup diced red onion

1. Preheat oven to 350° F. Heat first 3 ingredients on med. heat in saucepan.
2. Combine corn and veggies in oven-safe dish.
3. When cheese mixture has melted, pour over corn. Toss to coat well.
4. Bake for 45 minutes.

Country Baked Beans

SERVINGS 6 • PREP TIME 10 minutes • COOK TIME 30 minutes

- 5 slices bacon
- 2 15 oz. cans pinto beans
- 1 15 oz. can white kidney beans
- 1 15 oz. can navy beans
- 1 sm. onion, diced
- ¾ cup barbeque sauce
- ¼ cup brown sugar

1. Brown bacon till crispy; set aside.
2. Drain about half the juice from all the beans.
3. In lg. skillet, combine all ingredients and bring to a boil.
4. Reduce heat and cover; simmer for 20 minutes. Or place in 9" x 13" oven-safe dish and bake at 375° F. for 30 minutes.

Side Dishes

Crunchy Potato Bake

SERVINGS 4 • PREP TIME 15 minutes • COOK TIME 30 minutes

- 4 russet potatoes
- ½ cup butter
- 1 cup crushed Corn Flakes cereal
- 1½ cups shredded cheese
- 2 tsp. salt
- 1½ tsp. paprika

1. Preheat oven to 375° F. Wash potatoes. Cut in half lengthwise, then slice into ½-inch strips.

2. Melt butter on jelly roll sheet in oven. Coat potatoes with melted butter and spread out to a single layer.

3. Combine remaining ingredients and sprinkle over potatoes.

4. Bake for 30 minutes or until potatoes are crispy.

Easy Potato Casserole

SERVINGS 6 • PREP TIME 10 minutes • COOK TIME 1 hour

- 1 lg. pkg. frozen hash browns
- 12 oz. sour cream
- 1 can cream of celery soup
- 1 can cream of potato soup
- 1 tsp. dry minced onion (if desired)
- salt and pepper to taste

1. Preheat oven to 325° F. Mix all ingredients well in a lg. bowl and spread in lg. casserole dish.

2. Bake for 1 hour.

Green Bean Casserole

SERVINGS 6 • PREP TIME 10 minutes • COOK TIME 40 minutes

- ¾ cup milk
- 1 10 oz. can cream of mushroom soup
- ⅛ tsp. black pepper
- 2 9 oz pkgs. frozen green beans, thawed or 2 14 oz. cans of green beans, drained
- 1 3 oz. can French fried onions

1 Preheat oven to 350° F. In 2 qt. baking dish, combine milk, soup, and pepper. Stir in green beans and ½ of the fried onions.

2 Bake uncovered for 30 minutes. Remove from oven and stir. Sprinkle top with remaining fried onions and continue baking for 10 minutes or until hot and bubbly.

Green Bean Melody

SERVINGS 6 • PREP TIME 10 minutes • COOK TIME 20 minutes

- 1 cup chopped red bell peppers
- ¼ cup onion, finely chopped
- 1 Tbs. butter
- 1 can cream of celery soup
- ½ cup milk
- 1 tsp. Worcestershire sauce
- ⅛ tsp. hot pepper sauce
- 2 16 oz. bags frozen tiny whole green beans
- 1 8 oz. can water chestnuts, drained
- 1 cup shredded cheese

1 Preheat oven to 350° F. In a lg. skillet, sauté peppers and onions in butter until tender or onions are mostly clear.

2 Add soup, milk, Worcestershire sauce, and hot pepper sauce; stir until smooth.

3 Stir in green beans and water chestnuts. Transfer to an ungreased 2 qt. baking dish.

4 Sprinkle with cheese. Bake for 20 minutes, uncovered.

Homemade French Fries

SERVINGS 4 • PREP TIME 15 minutes • COOK TIME 20 minutes

- **4 lg. russet potatoes**
- **oil**
- **salt and pepper**

1 Wash potatoes and remove any defects. In electric fryer or lg. skillet, heat oil until hot.

2 Cut potatoes in half lengthwise, then cut into thin strips. You can use a potato cutter if you have one.

3 Place a handful of potatoes into the hot oil, stirring often for about 3 to 5 minutes. Remove from oil and place on paper towel to drain. This is called blanching.

4 Once all the potatoes are blanched and drained, begin to fry again in same oil. This time the potatoes will get brown and crisp.

5 As they are done, place potatoes on clean paper towel and sprinkle with salt and pepper to taste. (Salting potatoes while hot is key!)

Mashed Sweet Potatoes

SERVINGS 4 • PREP TIME 10 minutes • COOK TIME 20 minutes

- **4 med. yams**
- **¼ cup brown sugar**
- **2 Tbs. butter**
- **¼ cup milk**
- **salt and pepper to taste**

1 Peel yams and cook in lg. saucepan for about 20 minutes until tender. Drain.

2 In lg. bowl, add remaining ingredients. Beat with hand mixer until creamy. Serve warm.

Side Dishes

Mexican Coleslaw

SERVINGS 6 • PREP TIME 15 minutes • COOK TIME 0 minutes

- 6 cups cabbage, very thinly sliced
- 1½ cups carrots, peeled and grated
- ⅓ cup fresh cilantro, chopped
- ¼ cup rice vinegar
- 2 Tbs. extra virgin olive oil
- ¼ tsp. salt

1. Place cabbage and carrots in a colander; rinse thoroughly with cold water to crisp. Let drain 5 minutes.
2. Meanwhile, whisk cilantro, vinegar, oil, and salt in a lg. bowl. Add cabbage and carrots; toss well to coat.
3. To make this coleslaw even faster, use a coleslaw mix containing cabbage and carrots from the produce section of the supermarket.
4. Serve immediately or cover and refrigerate for up to 1 day. Toss again to refresh just before serving.

Old Fashioned Scalloped Potatoes

SERVINGS 4 • PREP TIME 20 minutes • COOK TIME 1 hour

- 4 med. potatoes, peeled and sliced thin
- salt and pepper to taste
- 3 Tbs. flour
- 4 Tbs. butter
- 1½ cups milk

1. Preheat oven to 350° F. Spray 1½ qt. casserole dish with cooking spray. Cover the bottom with single layer of potatoes. Sprinkle generously with salt and pepper.
2. Place ½ of the flour and butter over potatoes. Repeat until all the potatoes are used.
3. Pour milk over potatoes until top is almost covered.
4. Bake 1 hour or until potatoes are tender.

Oven Baked Fried Potatoes

SERVINGS 4 • PREP TIME 20 minutes • COOK TIME 20 minutes

- 5 to 6 med. potatoes
- 2 Tbs. olive oil
- ½ tsp. seasoning salt
- ⅛ tsp. black pepper

1 Preheat oven to 425° F. Wash potatoes and peel if desired. Slice in quarters and slice thin. Pour oil into lg. zip lock bag.

2 Add sliced potatoes and sprinkle with seasoning salt and pepper. Shake well.

3 Spread out on ungreased cookie sheet.

4 Bake for 20 minutes.

Oven Roasted Potatoes

SERVINGS 4 • PREP TIME 15 minutes • COOK TIME 40 minutes

- 1 envelope dry onion soup mix
- 4 red potatoes, washed and cut into lg. pieces
- ⅓ cup olive oil
- ¼ tsp. black pepper
- ½ tsp. season salt

1 Preheat oven to 450° F. Place all ingredients in lg. plastic bag. Toss to coat well.

2 Spread out on cookie sheets, being sure all potatoes are laying in a single layer.

3 Bake for 30 to 40 minutes, or until potatoes are tender.

Side Dishes

Party Potatoes

SERVINGS 6 • PREP TIME 5 minutes • COOK TIME 1 hours

- 1 to 2 lb. bag of hash browns
- 1 cup sour cream
- 1 can cream of chicken soup
- ½ cup butter, melted
- 2 cups Velveeta cheese, cubed
- 1 Tbs. minced onion
- ½ tsp. salt
- ¼ tsp. black pepper

1 Preheat oven to 350° F. Mix all ingredients and place in a shallow baking dish.

2 Bake for 1 hour or until golden brown.

Red Potatoes Baked or Grilled

SERVINGS 4 • PREP TIME 5 minutes • COOK TIME 40 minutes

- 1 sm. onion, thinly sliced
- 4 med. red potatoes cut in bite sized pieces
- 1 med. green bell pepper, cubed
- ½ cup Italian or ranch dressing
- ½ tsp. salt
- ¼ tsp. pepper

1 Preheat oven to 400° F. or grill on med high. Spray foil with nonstick spray. Center onion on 1 sheet heavy duty aluminum foil (18" x 24").

2 Combine potatoes, peppers, dressing, salt, and pepper; spread evenly over onions.

3 Bring up sides of foil and double fold. Double fold ends to form one lg. foil packet, leaving room for heat to circulate inside packet.

4 Bake 30 to 36 minutes on a cookie sheet or grill 15 to 20 minutes in covered grill.

Side Dishes

Red Beans & Rice

SERVINGS 6 • PREP TIME 10 minutes • COOK TIME 45 minutes

- 1 cup uncooked rice
- 1 16 ounce pkg. turkey kielbasa, cut diagonally into 1/4 inch slices
- 1 onion, chopped
- 1 green bell pepper, chopped
- 1 clove garlic, chopped
- 2 15 oz. cans canned kidney beans, drained
- 1 16 oz. can whole peeled tomatoes, chopped
- ½ tsp. dried oregano
- salt to taste
- ½ tsp. pepper

1. In a saucepan, bring water to a boil. Add rice and stir. Reduce heat, cover, and simmer for 20 minutes.
2. In a lg. skillet over low heat, cook sausage for 5 minutes.
3. Stir in onion, green pepper, and garlic; sauté until tender.
4. Pour in beans and tomatoes with juice. Season with oregano, salt, and pepper.
5. Simmer uncovered for 20 minutes. Serve over rice.

Spanish Rice

SERVINGS 6 • PREP TIME 10 minutes • COOK TIME 6 hours in slow cooker

- 1½ cups long grain rice
- ½ cup olive oil or butter
- 1½ cups tomato juice
- 1½ cups water
- 1 onion, finely chopped
- 1 green bell pepper, finely chopped
- 1½ tsp. salt
- 1 lb. ground beef, browned and drained

1. Sauté rice in oil until golden brown. Place in slow cooker with remaining ingredients.
2. Stir well. Cover and cook on low for 4 to 6 hours. (High 2 to 3 hours)

Spinach Soufflé

SERVINGS 6 • PREP TIME 10 minutes • COOK TIME 30 minutes

- 1 10 oz. pkg. frozen chopped spinach
- ⅓ cup finely chopped onions
- 2 eggs, separated
- ½ cup milk
- ½ cup shredded sharp cheddar cheese
- ½ cup bread crumbs or crushed crackers
- ¼ tsp. salt
- ⅛ tsp. black pepper

1. Preheat oven to 350° F. Defrost spinach; combine with onions, egg yolks, milk, cheese, bread crumbs. and seasonings.

2. In separate bowl, beat egg whites until stiff peaks form. Fold egg whites into spinach mixture.

3. Turn into casserole or soufflé dish.

4. Bake for 20 to 30 minutes.

Twice Baked Potatoes

SERVINGS 6 • PREP TIME 5 minutes • COOK TIME 1 hour

- 4 lg. russet potatoes
- ½ cup shredded cheese
- ½ cup sour cream
- 3 Tbs. milk
- ¼ cup butter
- salt and pepper
- 1 jar pimentos

1 Preheat oven to 425° F. Wash potatoes and wrap in foil. Bake for 45 minutes. Remove foil and cut each potato in half lengthwise.

2 Spoon out center of potatoes and place in med. mixing bowl. Place skins on a baking sheet.

3 Combine potato with cheese, sour cream, milk, butter, salt, pepper, and pimentos. Mix until blended. (It will be lumpy.)

4 Fill each potato skin with filling. Sprinkle additional cheese over top.

5 Bake 15 minutes or until hot.

Wagon Wheel Pasta with Salsa-Marinated Beans

SERVINGS 6 • PREP TIME 5 minutes • COOK TIME 20 minutes

- 1 12 oz. jar of salsa
- 1 15 oz. can reduced-sodium black beans, rinsed and drained
- ½ cup frozen corn kernels, defrosted
- 2 Tbs. fresh lime juice
- 1 Tbs. olive oil
- ¼ tsp. salt
- ¼ tsp. fresh ground black pepper
- ½ tsp. ground cumin
- ½ cup low-fat feta cheese
- 2 cups wagon-wheel pasta
- ¼ cup finely chopped cilantro or parsley

1 Bring lg. pot of water to a boil for pasta. In lg. bowl, stir together salsa, black beans, corn, lime juice, olive oil, salt, pepper, cumin, and feta.

2 Let marinate at room temperature while waiting for the water to boil and the pasta to cook.

3 Put the pasta into boiling water and cook according to package directions.

4 Drain and stir into the salsa mixture. Stir in cilantro and serve.

NOTES

Desserts

Cookies

Almond Glazed Sugar Cookies	125
Butterscotch-Chocolate Chip Cookies	134
Cake Mix Cookies	134
Chocolate-Chip Cookies	126
Chocolate Coconut Balls	126
Coconut Islands Cookies	127
Cowboy Cookies	128
Gluten Free Peanut Butter Cookies	128
Grandma's Favorite Sugar Cookies	129
Lazy Boy Sugar Cookies	129
Oatmeal Chocolate-Chip Cookies	130
Oreo Truffles	130
Peanut Blossoms	131
Peanut Butter Cookies	131
Pumpkin-Orange Cookies	132
Rolled Sugar Cookies	133
Snicker Doodles	127

Cakes

Apple Cake	135
Berry Chocolate Cream Cake	136
Black Forest Cake	137
Carrot Cake	138
Cherry Cheesecake	139
Chocolate Cake with Raspberry Sauce	139
Country Apple Cake with Caramel Sauce	140
Dump Cake	142

Low-Calorie, Low-Fat Cake	142
Mayonnaise Cake	143
Mocha Pudding Cake	143
Orange Kiss-Me Cake	144
Oreo Cheesecake	144
Pumpkin Spice Cake	145
Red Velvet Cupcakes	146
Red Velvet Pound Cake	147
Rhubarb Surprise Cake	148
Rhubarb Upside Down Cake	148
Rhubarb Cake	147
Snowball Cake	149
Sweet Potato Cake	150
Triple Chocolate Triple Layer Cake	151

Frostings

7-Minute Frosting	152
Butter Cream Frosting	152
Chocolate Frosting	153
Chocolate Glaze	153
Coconut Pecan Frosting	154
Cream Cheese Frosting	154
Creamy Chocolate Frosting	155
Fluffy-As-a-Cloud Frosting	156
Light, Creamy Frosting	155
No-Weep Meringue	156

Almond Glazed Sugar Cookies

SERVINGS 18 cookies • PREP TIME 10 minutes • COOK TIME 7 – 9 minutes

- 1 cup butter
- ¾ cup granulated sugar
- 2 tsp. almond extract, divided
- 2 cups self-rising flour
- ¼ tsp. salt
- 1½ cups powdered sugar
- 4 to 5 Tbs. water
- sliced almonds (small pkg.)

1 Preheat oven to 400° F. In lg. mixing bowl, combine butter, sugar, and 1 tsp. almond extract. Beat at med. speed, scraping bowl often, until creamy (1 to 2 minutes).

2 Reduce speed to low, mix salt with flour, then slowly add flour mixture. Beat until well mixed.

3 Roll dough into 1 inch balls: place 2 inches apart on ungreased cookie sheet.

4 Flatten balls with bottom of a buttered glass dipped in sugar, until each is ¼ inch thick.

5 Bake for 7 to 9 minutes. Edges will be slightly brown. Cool 1 minute before removing from pan.

6 In small bowl, combine powdered sugar, 1 tsp. almond extract, and water, whisk well. Decorate each cookie with the glaze and sliced almonds.

To flatten drop cookies, use a glass with its bottom greased, then dipped in flour.

Desserts

Chocolate-Chip Cookies

SERVINGS 24 cookies • PREP TIME 10 minutes • COOK TIME 10 – 12 minutes

- 1 cup butter flavor Crisco
- 1 cup firmly packed brown sugar
- ½ cup sugar
- 2 eggs
- 1 tsp. vanilla
- 2½ cups self-rising flour
- 12 oz. chocolate chips

1 Preheat oven to 375° F. In mixer or lg. bowl, beat Crisco until smooth. Add sugars and beat well. Add eggs and vanilla; beat until well blended.

2 Slowly add flour. When mixed well, stir in chocolate chips with wooden spoon.

3 Place by rounded teaspoons onto ungreased cookie sheet.

4 Bake for 10 to 12 minutes. Remove from cookie sheet while hot: place on wire rack.

Chocolate Coconut Balls

SERVINGS 12 cookies • PREP TIME 10 minutes • COOK TIME 15 minutes

- 3 Baker's chocolate squares
- 2 Tbs. butter
- 1 cup powdered sugar
- 1 egg, beaten
- 1 cup chopped nuts
- 1 sm. pkg. mini marshmallows
- 1 bag coconut flakes

1 Melt 3 chocolate squares with 2 Tbs. butter. Add powdered sugar and egg. Add nuts and mini marshmallows.

2 Form into balls. Put coconut flakes on waxed paper and roll cookies in coconut. Place on serving tray. Cool before serving.

To toast coconut or nuts, bake at 375° F. for 5 to 7 minutes, stirring occasionally until golden brown.

Desserts

Coconut Islands Cookies

SERVINGS 24 cookies • **PREP TIME** 10 minutes • **COOK TIME** 12 – 15 minutes

- 3 oz. unsweetened chocolate chips, melted
- 1 tsp. instant coffee
- ½ cup butter, softened
- 1 cup firmly packed brown sugar
- 1 egg
- ½ cup sour cream
- 2 cups self-rising flour
- 1 cup coconut flakes

Frosting:
- 2 oz. unsweetened chocolate chips, melted
- ¼ cup sour cream
- 2 cups powdered sugar

1 Preheat oven to 375° F. In lg. mixing bowl, combine all except ½ cup of the coconut. Beat at lowest speed until all is well blended.

2 Drop dough by rounded teaspoonfuls onto greased cookie sheets.

3 Bake for 12 to 15 minutes. Frost while warm, then sprinkle with remaining coconut.

4 Frosting: Combine melted chocolate chips with sour cream and powdered sugar. Blend until smooth.

Snicker Doodles

SERVINGS 24 cookies • **PREP TIME** 5 minutes • **COOK TIME** 8 – 10 minutes

- 1½ cups sugar
- 1 stick butter
- 2 eggs
- 2¾ cups self-rising flour
- 2 tsp. cream of tartar
- ¼ cup sugar
- 2 tsp. cinnamon

1 Preheat oven to 400° F. Combine all ingredients through cream of tartar until well blended.

2 In small bowl, combine ¼ cup sugar and 2 tsp. cinnamon.

3 Drop cookie dough by spoonfuls into bowl and roll to cover cookies.

4 Place on ungreased cookie sheet and bake for 8 to 10 minutes.

5 Remove from cookie sheet immediately and place on wire racks.

Cowboy Cookies

SERVINGS 24 cookies • **PREP TIME** 15 minutes • **COOK TIME** 12 minutes

- 2 cups self-rising flour
- 2 cups quick oats
- ½ tsp. cinnamon
- 1 cup sugar
- 1 cup brown sugar
- 1 cup butter
- 2 eggs
- 1 tsp. vanilla
- 1 cup semi-sweet chocolate chips
- 1½ cups chopped pecans

1. Preheat oven to 350° F. Toss flour, oats, and cinnamon in a bowl; set aside.
2. In lg. mixing bowl, combine sugars with butter and add eggs and vanilla. Stir in flour and oats mixture.
3. Stir in chocolate chips and nuts until well blended. Form into walnut-size balls with lightly floured hands.
4. Flatten with bottom of a glass that is lightly floured. This will help cookies be more uniform in shape.
5. Bake 9 to 12 minutes. Edges will be slightly brown. You don't want to overcook.

Gluten-Free Peanut Butter Cookies

SERVINGS 12 cookies • **PREP TIME** 5 minutes • **COOK TIME** 15 minutes

- 1 cup crunchy peanut butter
- 1 cup + ¼ cup sugar
- 1 egg
- 12 Hershey's Kisses

1. Preheat oven to 370° F. Mix peanut butter, 1 cup sugar, and egg. Shape into 1 inch balls.
2. Place ¼ cup sugar in a small mixing bowl and roll each cookie dough in the sugar lightly. Place on ungreased cookie sheet.
3. Bake for 12 to 15 minutes. Remove from oven when edges start to brown.
4. Press a Kiss into center of each cookie while still hot.

Desserts

Grandma's Favorite Sugar Cookies

SERVINGS 36 cookies • **PREP TIME** 10 minutes • **COOK TIME** 10 minutes

- 1 cup shortening
- 2 cups sugar
- 1 cup sour cream
- 3 eggs
- 1 tsp. vanilla
- 1 tsp. baking soda
- 1 tsp. baking powder
- ½ tsp. nutmeg
- ½ tsp. cinnamon
- ⅛ tsp. mace
- 5½ to 6 cups flour
- additional sugar

1 Preheat oven to 350° F. Cream shortening and sugar. Add sour cream, eggs, and vanilla.

2 In separate bowl, combine dry ingredients. Add into wet mixture. Chill one hour or overnight. Take out half of dough at a time, leaving other half in refrigerator.

3 Use a cookie scoop to form cookies, then roll in sugar and place on ungreased cookie sheet.

4 Bake for 8 to 10 minutes. Baking for 8 minutes will give a softer cookie; 10 minutes will give a crisper cookie.

Lazy Boy Sugar Cookies

SERVINGS 24 cookies • **PREP TIME** 5 minutes • **COOK TIME** 10 – 12 minutes

- 1 stick butter flavor Crisco
- ½ cup sugar
- ½ cup powdered sugar
- 1½ tsp. vanilla
- 1 egg
- 2¼ cups self-rising flour
- ½ tsp. cream of tartar

1 Preheat oven to 350° F. Mix all ingredients until smooth. Roll into 1 inch balls and place on ungreased cookie sheet.

2 Press with bottom of a glass dipped in sugar.

3 Bake for 10 to 12 minutes, or until edges are lightly brown.

Desserts

Oatmeal Chocolate-Chip Cookies

SERVINGS 48 cookies • PREP TIME 10 minutes • COOK TIME 12–15 minutes

- ¾ cup butter flavor Crisco
- 1 cup brown sugar
- ½ cup granulated sugar
- ½ tsp. ground cinnamon
- ¼ tsp. ground cloves
- 2 eggs
- 1 tsp. vanilla
- 2 cups rolled oats
- 1½ cups self-rising flour
- 1½ cups chocolate chips

1. Preheat oven to 370° F. Beat Crisco until creamy; add sugars, cinnamon, and cloves and blend well. Beat in eggs and vanilla until well blended.

2. Add oats and flour alternately until all is mixed in. Fold in chocolate chips.

3. Using a cookie scoop, drop rounded cookie balls onto ungreased cookie sheet.

4. Bake for 12 to 15 minutes. Cookies are done when edges are slightly brown.

5. Remove from cookie sheet immediately and place on wire rack. Store in airtight container.

Variety: Substitute raisins for chocolate chips.

Oreo Truffles

SERVINGS 48 cookies • PREP TIME 15 minutes • COOK TIME 0 minutes

- 1 8 oz. cream cheese, softened
- 4½ cups Oreo cookies, finely crushed
- 2 pkgs. chocolate squares, melted

1. Mix cream cheese and Oreos until well blended.

2. Shape into 48 balls. Dip each in melted chocolate; place on wax paper.

3. Sprinkle with remaining crumbs while cookies are wet. Refrigerate about an hour.

Peanut Blossoms

SERVINGS 36 cookies • PREP TIME 10 minutes • COOK TIME 10 – 12 minutes

- 1¾ cups self-rising flour
- ½ cup sugar
- ½ cup packed brown sugar
- ½ cup shortening
- ½ cup peanut butter

- 1 egg
- 2 Tbs. milk
- 1 tsp. vanilla
- 48 candy kisses

1. Preheat oven to 375° F. Combine all ingredients except Kisses, in lg. mixing bowl. Mix on low speed until dough forms.

2. Shape into balls, using a rounded teaspoon or cookie scoop. Roll each ball into sugar; place on ungreased cookie sheet.

3. Bake for 10 to 12 minutes.

4. Top each cookie with a Kiss while still warm, pressing down firmly so each cookie cracks around the edges.

Peanut Butter Cookies

SERVINGS 36 cookies • PREP TIME 5 minutes • COOK TIME 14 minutes

- 1 cup crunchy peanut butter
- 1 cup butter flavor Crisco
- 1 cup brown sugar
- 1 cup sugar

- 2 eggs
- 1 tsp. vanilla
- 2½ cups self-rising flour
- 1 cup granulated sugar

1. Preheat oven to 370° F. Cream peanut butter and Crisco; add sugars. Blend eggs and vanilla in well.

2. Stir in flour slowly until all is worked in. Dough will be soft.

3. Place 1 cup sugar in small mixing bowl. Drop cookie dough into sugar and roll gently. Place on ungreased cookies sheet, leaving space for spreading.

4. Use a fork dipped in the sugar to press crisscross marks onto each cookie.

5. Bake for 14 minutes. Cookies are done when edges start to turn brown. Cookies will be soft until they fully cool.

6. Remove from cookie sheet to wire rack immediately. Store in airtight container.

Desserts

Pumpkin-Orange Cookies

SERVINGS 24 cookies • PREP TIME 10 minutes • COOK TIME 12 – 14 minutes

- 1 cup butter, softened
- 1 cup sugar
- ½ cup packed brown sugar
- 1 egg
- 15 oz. can pumpkin
- 2 Tbs. orange juice
- 1 tsp. grated orange peel
- 2½ cups self-rising flour
- ½ cup chopped nuts (optional)

Glaze:
- ½ cup sifted powdered sugar
- 2 to 3 Tbs. orange juice
- ½ tsp. grated orange peel

1 Preheat oven to 375° F. Beat butter and sugars in lg. bowl until creamy. Add egg, pumpkin, orange juice, and peel, beating until combined well.

2 Gradually add flour until well blended. Stir in nuts.

3 Drop dough by rounded tablespoons onto ungreased baking sheet.

4 Bake for 12 to 14 minutes, or until edges are set.

5 Remove to wire racks to cool completely.

6 To make glaze, combine powdered sugar, orange juice, and grated orange peel until smooth. Spread ½ tsp. of glaze over each cookie.

Double your cookie recipes and use one batch for later. Put un-cooked cookies on waxed paper covered cookie sheets and freeze. After they are frozen, place in freezer bags. You can pull out a few cookies at a time.

Desserts

Rolled Sugar Cookies

SERVINGS varies depending on cookie cutter sizes
PREP TIME 30 minutes • COOK TIME 8 minutes

- 1 cup sugar
- 1 cup butter flavor Crisco
- 1 tsp. vanilla
- 2 cups self-rising flour
- ½ tsp. cream of tarter
- 1 egg
- 1 Tbs. milk

Frosting:
- 4 cups powdered sugar
- ¼ cup milk
- ½ tsp. vanilla
- food coloring
- sprinkles

1 Preheat oven to 350° F. Mix well all ingredients through milk in lg. bowl. Roll ¼ of the dough out on wax paper covered lightly with flour.

2 Roll out to 1/4" thickness. Cut out with favorite cookie cutters.

3 Place on ungreased cookie sheet. Bake 8 minutes, until edges are just brown. Cool on wire rack.

4 Make frosting by combining powdered sugar with vanilla, adding in milk a few drops at a time until it reaches the right consistency, keeping it a little thick. Divide into 4 bowls.

5 Add food coloring to each bowl. Frost cookies and add sprinkles while frosting is still wet. Set aside until fully dry.

Butterscotch-Chocolate Chip Cookies

SERVINGS 24 cookies • PREP TIME 10 minutes • COOK TIME 12 minutes

- 1 cup sugar
- 1 cup butter flavor Crisco
- 2 eggs
- 1 tsp. vanilla
- 2 cups self-rising flour
- 2 cups quick oats
- ½ cup butterscotch chips
- ½ cup semi-sweet chocolate chips
- ½ cup chopped walnuts

1. Preheat oven to 350° F. In lg. mixing bowl, combine sugar and Crisco. Add eggs and vanilla; mix well.
2. Slowly stir in flour and oats. Stir in butterscotch chips, chocolate chips, and walnuts.
3. Roll into walnut-size balls. Place on ungreased cookie sheet.
4. Bake for 12 minutes. Cool on wire rack.

Cake Mix Cookies

SERVINGS 24 cookies • PREP TIME 5 minutes • COOK TIME 10 minutes

- 1 box of any flavor cake mix
- ⅓ cup oil
- 2 eggs
- ½ cup flour

1. Preheat oven to 350° F. Mix ingredients together. Drop by spoonfuls on cookie sheet sprayed with cooking spray.
2. Bake for 8 to 10 minutes. Cool on wire rack.

Apple Cake

SERVINGS 12 • PREP TIME 15 minutes • COOK TIME 1½ – 1¾ hours

- 3 Tbs. sugar
- 3 tsp. ground cinnamon, divided
- 3 cups self-rising flour
- ¼ tsp. ground nutmeg
- 2 cups sugar
- 1½ cups canola oil
- 3 eggs
- 3 Granny Smith apples, peeled and chopped
- 2 tsp. vanilla
- 1 cup chopped pecans
- ½ cup raisins
- 1 can of vanilla frosting

Glaze:
- 1½ cup packed brown sugar
- ½ cup butter
- ½ cup chopped pecans
- 3 Tbs. milk

1. Preheat oven to 325° F. Grease 10" tube pan. In small bowl, combine 3 Tbs. sugar and 1 tsp. of the cinnamon. Coat tube pan with the sugar mixture.

2. In med. bowl at med. speed, combine flour, nutmeg, and remaining cinnamon. Set aside.

3. In lg. bowl, mix sugar and oil until well blended. Beat in eggs one at a time. Stir in apples and vanilla.

4. Stir in flour mixture and mix until well blended. Stir in pecans and raisins.

5. Spread into prepared pan. Lift slightly and drop onto counter to remove air bubbles.

6. Bake for 1½ to 1¾ hours. Poke toothpick in the center: if it comes out clean cake is done.

7. Prepare glaze and drizzle over cake while cake is warm.

Desserts

Berry Chocolate Cream Cake

SERVINGS 12 • PREP TIME 20 minutes • COOK TIME 30 – 35 minutes

- 1 pkg. angel food cake mix
- ¼ cup unsweetened cocoa powder
- ¼ cup coffee-flavor liqueur
- 5 cups Cool Whip, thawed
- 1 pt. strawberries, sliced
- **Chocolate dipped strawberries** (optional)

1 Position oven rack in lower third of oven; preheat to 350° F.

2 In glass bowl, stir cake mix and cocoa powder until lump free. At low speed, beat in liqueur and 1 cup water until moistened, 1 to 2 minutes.

3 Increase speed to med.; beat 1 minute. Spoon cake evenly into 10" ungreased angel food cake pan.

4 Bake 30 to 35 minutes or until toothpick inserted comes out clean. Invert onto bottle or lg. funnel; cool completely, about 1 hour.

5 Remove cake from pan, loosening edges with knife if needed. Invert onto platter. Horizontally cut top ⅓ of cake top.

6 Using small knife, cut tunnel out of cake, leaving 1 inch thickness on inside wall, and 1½ inch thickness on outside wall.

7 Pull out cake from tunnel center and discard. Fold strawberries into 2 cups Cool Whip: spread into center of cake.

8 Replace cake top, pressing lightly to adhere. Spread Cool Whip on top and sides of cake as a frosting. Garnish with chocolate-dipped strawberries.

To fold in: to combine ingredients with a spoon, whisk or fork. Cut down through the mixture, slice tool under the mixture and bring over the top gently.

Desserts

Black Forest Cake

SERVINGS 10–12 • PREP TIME 20 minutes • COOK TIME 28 minutes

- 1 box chocolate cake mix
- 2 20 oz. cans tart, pitted cherries
- 1 cup sugar
- ¼ cup cornstarch
- 1½ tsp. vanilla
- 3 cups whipped cream
- ⅓ cup powdered sugar

1. Bake cake mix as directed on box for 2-layer cake; let cool.

2. Drain cherries, reserving ½ cup liquid. Combine juice, cherries, and sugar with cornstarch in small saucepan. Cook over low heat until thick.

3. Remove from heat, stir in vanilla.

4. Split each cake layer horizontally. Crumble one half of one of the cakes, set aside

5. Mix whipped cream and sugar and spread over one layer of cake. Top with ⅓ cup cherries.

6. Layer same with other two layers of cake, ending with whipped cream. Pat top and sides of cake with crumbled cake pieces on top and sides.

7. Garnish with cherries on top.

Carrot Cake

SERVINGS 12 • PREP TIME 20 minutes • COOK TIME 45 minutes

- 2 cups sugar
- 1½ cups oil
- 4 eggs
- 2 tsp. vanilla
- 3 cups self-rising flour
- 2 tsp. cinnamon
- 2 cups shredded carrots
- 1 small can crushed pineapple
- 2 cup chopped nuts, divided

Frosting:
- 3 cups powdered sugar
- 1 8 oz. pkg. cream cheese
- 2 Tbs. butter
- 1 tsp. vanilla
- Candy corn to garnish (optional)

1. Preheat oven to 350° F. Combine sugar, oil, eggs, and vanilla in mixer bowl. Beat on med. for 2 minutes.

2. In lg. bowl, combine flour and cinnamon; combine with liquid mixture and blend well.

3. Stir in carrots, pineapple, and 1 cup chopped nuts.

4. Pour into three floured and sprayed 8-inch round cake pans.

5. Bake for 45 minutes or until toothpick comes out clean. Cool completely.

6. For frosting, beat powdered sugar, cream cheese, butter, and vanilla until fluffy and smooth. Frost cake.

7. Sprinkle chopped nuts over the top and place candy corn on as garnish.

Drain maraschino cherries, crushed pineapples and other fruits thoroughly on absorbent paper towel.

Desserts

Cherry Cheesecake

SERVINGS 8 • PREP TIME 5 minutes • COOK TIME 0 minutes

- 16 oz. cream cheese
- 1 can sweetened condensed milk
- ⅓ cup lemon juice
- 1 tsp. vanilla
- 1 graham cracker pie crust
- 1 can of cherry pie filling

1 Beat cream cheese until creamy; add condensed milk slowly,

2 Stir in lemon juice and vanilla until well mixed.

3 Pour into pie crust. Add cherries on top and refrigerate for 2 hours.

Chocolate Cake with Raspberry Sauce

SERVINGS 12 • PREP TIME 10 minutes • COOK TIME 35 minutes

- 2 cups self-rising flour
- 1½ cups granulated sugar
- 1½ cups buttermilk
- ⅔ cup unsweetened cocoa powder
- 1 cup butter, softened
- 2 eggs
- 1½ tsp. vanilla
- 2 cups frozen raspberries, thawed
- 2 Tbs. sugar
- 1 Tbs. cornstarch
- fresh raspberries
- mint leaves for garnish

1 Preheat oven to 350° F. In lg. mixing bowl, combine flour, 1½ cups sugar, buttermilk, cocoa, butter, eggs, and vanilla. Beat on low speed just until blended.

2 Beat on high speed 3 minutes. Spread batter onto 9" x 13" baking dish, lightly sprayed with cooking spray.

3 Bake for 30 to 35 minutes or until cake tests done with toothpick. Cool on wire rack.

4 Cut into 16 squares.

5 For glaze, puree raspberries in electric blender until smooth. Strain off seeds. In small saucepan, combine raspberries with sugar and cornstarch. Cook until thickened and comes to a boil. Chill, then place on cake.

6 Place two or three raspberries on top of each piece of cake with and two mint sprigs, if desired, for garnish.

Desserts

Country Apple Cake with Caramel Sauce

SERVINGS 12 • PREP TIME 10 minutes • COOK TIME 55 minutes

- 2 Tbs. oil
- 1 egg
- 1 pkg. Pillsbury Nut or Cranberry Quick Bread mix
- 2 cans apple pie filling
- 2 tsp. ground cinnamon
- ½ tsp. nutmeg
- ½ cup chopped walnuts

Sauce:
- ½ cup sugar
- ½ cup firmly packed brown sugar
- ½ cup butter
- ½ cup whipping cream
- 1 tsp. vanilla

1 Preheat oven to 325° F. Spray 9" x 13" baking dish with non-stick cooking spray.

2 In lg. mixing bowl, beat oil and egg well. Add bread mix, apple pie filling, cinnamon, and nutmeg. Stir until mix is moistened.

3 Stir in nuts. Spoon into prepared pan and bake for 45 to 55 minutes. Test with toothpick inserted into center; if it comes out clean it is done.

4 While cake is baking, prepare sauce. In a med. saucepan mix sugars, butter, and cream. Bring to a boil, stirring occasionally. Remove from heat and add vanilla.

5 To serve, cut warm cake into squares and place on individual plates. Top each serving with warm sauce. Add Cool Whip or ice cream, if desired.

To soften almonds and brazil nuts for slicing, soak a few minutes in boiling water.

Desserts

Drummer Boy Cake

SERVINGS 12 • PREP TIME 30 minutes • COOK TIME 30 minutes

- 8 oz. Cool Whip (keep frozen)
- 1 chocolate cake mix
- 1 sm. box instant chocolate pudding
- ¼ cup plus 2 Tbs. powdered sugar
- ½ tsp. milk
- 11 vanilla wafers
- 4 squares semi-sweet chocolate, chopped
- 8 oz. cream cheese, softened
- 10 oz. jar maraschino cherries
- 1 strip Red Vine licorice
- 2 marshmallows
- 2 pretzel rods

1 Put 1/3 of Cool Whip in bowl, set aside and freeze the remainder. Prepare cake batter as directed on package; blend in pudding mix. Bake as directed in two 9-inch round layer pans. Cool cake in pans for 10 minutes, then invert onto wire racks. Cool completely.

2 Mix 2 Tbs. powdered sugar with milk. Brush onto wafers.

3 Microwave remaining Cool Whip with chopped chocolate on high for 1½ minutes or until chocolate is melted, stirring after 1 minute. Cool 15 minutes to thicken.

4 Whisk cream cheese and remaining sugar until blended. Stir in cherries and thawed, reserved Cool Whip.

5 Stack cake on serving platter, filling with cream cheese mixture between layers. Frost with chocolate mixture.

6 Decorate with wafers around sides of cake. Place licorice around edge of cake on top and lower edges to look like a drum.

7 Place a marshmallow on end of each pretzel rod to look like a drum stick. Lay sticks on top of the cake across each other.

Always preheat oven before baking.

Desserts

Dump Cake

SERVINGS 12 • PREP TIME 5 minutes • COOK TIME 30 minutes

- 1 yellow cake mix
- 1 lg. can peaches, cherries, or apples
- ¼ cup melted butter
- nuts (optional)
- Cool Whip (optional)

1 Preheat oven to 375° F. Place fruit in bottom of 9" x 13" pan; sprinkle dry cake mix over fruit.

2 Drizzle butter over the top of dry cake mix. Top with nuts if desired before baking.

3 Bake for 30 minutes. Serve warm, topped with Cool Whip.

Low-Calorie, Low-Fat Cake

SERVINGS 6–8 • PREP TIME 5 minutes • COOK TIME 28 minutes

- 1 cake mix
- 1 can diet soda
- Cool Whip

1 Preheat oven to 350° F. Beat cake mix and soda for 2 minutes.

2 Spray two 8" round cake pans with cooking spray and coat with flour.

3 Pour batter into pans and bake for 28 minutes; cool completely.

4 Frost with Cool Whip.

(With yellow or white cake, use diet Sprite. With chocolate cake, use diet Coke.)

Desserts

Mayonnaise Cake

SERVINGS 12 • PREP TIME 10 minutes • COOK TIME 30 minutes

- ¼ cup unsweetened cocoa powder
- 2 cups flour
- 1 cup sugar
- 2 tsp. baking soda
- 1 cup cold water
- 1 cup mayonnaise

1 Preheat oven to 360° F. Combine all ingredients and blend until smooth and well blended.

2 Pour into 9" x 13" baking pan, sprayed with cooking spray.

3 Bake for 25 to 30 minutes or until toothpick stuck in the center comes out clean.

Mocha Pudding Cake

SERVINGS 12 • PREP TIME 25 minutes • COOK TIME 55 minutes

- 1 Tbs. instant coffee
- 1 cup water
- 4 eggs
- ¼ cup oil
- 1 box yellow cake mix
- 3 oz. box instant chocolate pudding

Glaze:
- 1 tsp. instant coffee
- 2 Tbs. milk
- 1½ cups powdered sugar
- ¼ tsp. vanilla
- dash of salt

1 Preheat oven to 350° F. Dissolve coffee in water. Combine remaining ingredients in lg. mixing bowl and add coffee. Blend well.

2 Mix at med. speed for 2 minutes. Pour into greased and floured 10-inch Bundt pan or tube pan.

3 Bake for 50 to 55 minutes. Cool in pan for 15 minutes.

4 Make coffee glaze: Dissolve instant coffee in milk in a bowl. Blend in powdered sugar, vanilla, and a dash of salt. Drizzle over warm cake.

Orange Kiss-Me Cake

SERVINGS 12 • PREP TIME 10 minutes • COOK TIME 45 minutes

- 6 oz. frozen orange juice, thawed
- 2 cups self-rising flour
- 1 cup sugar
- ½ cup shortening
- ½ cup milk
- 2 eggs
- 1 cup raisins
- ⅓ cup chopped walnuts

Topping
- ⅓ cup sugar
- ¼ cup chopped walnuts
- 1 tsp. ground cinnamon

1. Preheat oven to 350° F. Spray 9" x 13" pan with cooking spray.

2. Combine ⅓ cup orange juice concentrate with remaining cake ingredients in lg. mixing bowl.

3. Blend at lowest speed for 30 seconds. Beat 3 minutes at med. speed. Pour into prepared pan.

4. Bake for 40 to 45 minutes. Drizzle remaining orange juice concentrate over warm cake.

5. Combine topping ingredients and sprinkle over cake.

Oreo Cheesecake

SERVINGS 8 • PREP TIME 15 minutes • COOK TIME 45 minutes; chill 3 hours

- 2 8 oz. pkg. cream cheese
- ½ cup sugar
- ½ tsp. vanilla
- 2 eggs
- 12 Oreo cookies, crushed
- 1 9" graham cracker pie crust

1. Preheat oven to 350° F. In lg. mixing bowl, combine cream cheese and sugar until smooth.

2. Add vanilla and eggs and mix until well combined. Gently stir in crushed cookies.

3. Pour into pie crust. Bake for 45 minutes.

4. Refrigerate 3 hours or overnight.

Desserts

Pumpkin Spice Cake

SERVINGS 12 • PREP TIME 10 minutes • COOK TIME 1 hour

- ¾ cups butter
- 2 cups granulated sugar
- 3 eggs
- 1½ cups canned pumpkin
- 1 cup sour milk *
- 1½ cups self-rising flour
- 1 Tbs. pumpkin pie spice

1. Preheat oven to 350° F. Prepare cake pan of your choosing, 9" x 13" or two 9-inch round pans. Spray with cooking spray and lightly flour.

2. Cream butter and sugar until well blended. Add eggs one at a time, blending after each addition.

3. In med. mixing bowl, blend pumpkin and milk well. In another bowl, mix flour and pumpkin spice.

4. Combine the three bowls alternately, mixing after each addition.

5. Bake for 55 to 60 minutes. Test if done by inserting toothpick into center of cake. If it comes out clean, it is done.

6. Cool completely on wire rack. Frost with Cream Cheese Frosting (page 154) or Butter Cream Frosting (page 152).

*To make sour milk, mix 1 cup milk and 1 tsp. lemon juice. Let sit at room temperature until ready to use.

Desserts

Red Velvet Cupcakes

SERVINGS 16 cupcakes • **PREP TIME** 10 minutes • **COOK TIME** 25 minutes

- 1 box red velvet cake mix
- 1 3 oz. package instant chocolate pudding

Frosting:
- 1 8 oz. pkg. of cream cheese, softened
- ½ cup butter, softened
- 4 cups powdered sugar
- 1 cup Cool Whip, thawed
- 1 square Baker's white chocolate, shaved

1 Prepare cake as directed; whisk in pudding mix.

2 Prepare cupcake pan with paper liners sprayed with cooking spray. Spoon batter into cupcake liners.

3 Bake as directed. Cool. (You can put them in the freezer and save them for later).

4 Once cooled, cut the center of each cupcake out to fill with frosting.

5 Prepare frosting: In med. size bowl, beat cream cheese and butter until well blended. Gradually beat in sugar. Whisk in Cool Whip.

6 Spoon frosting into lg. plastic bag, cut small corner off the bag. Squeeze frosting into each center of the cupcake.

7 Sprinkle white chocolate shavings over each cupcake. Keep refrigerated until serving.

To frost cupcakes quickly, put frosting in large bowl, add milk or water if necessary to make creamy, dip cooked cupcakes upside down in frosting, twirl and flip up quickly.

Desserts

Red Velvet Pound Cake

SERVINGS 12 • PREP TIME 10 minutes • COOK TIME 25 – 28 minutes

- 1 box yellow cake mix
- ½ cup oil
- 5 eggs
- 1 cup low-fat buttermilk
- 2 Tbs. cocoa
- 2 oz. red food coloring

Icing:
- 1 8 oz. pkg. cream cheese
- ¼ cup butter
- 1 box powdered sugar plus 2 Tbs.
- 1 tsp. vanilla

1. Prepare 9" x 13" pan by spraying with cooking spray.

2. In med. bowl, combine cake mix, oil, eggs, buttermilk, cocoa, and food coloring. Pour into pan and bake as directed on box.

3. Prepare icing: Cream cream cheese and butter. Slowly stir in powdered sugar and vanilla. Add a few drops of milk, if needed.

Rhubarb Cake

SERVINGS 12 • PREP TIME 10 minutes • COOK TIME 1 hour

- 4 cups chopped rhubarb
- 1 cup sugar
- 1 pint whipping cream, whipped
- 1 lemon flavored cake mix

1. Prepare cake as directed on package. Pour into 9" x 13" pan, sprayed with cooking spray.

2. Sprinkle rhubarb over top of cake and sprinkle sugar over rhubarb. Spread whipping cream over the top of the rhubarb.

3. It will look like you have done something wrong, but you didn't!

4. Bake at 350° F. for 50 to 60 minutes. Cake will be done when it springs back when touched in the center.

5. The cream and rhubarb will settle on the bottom as cake bakes; it will form a layer like custard. Serve warm. Refrigerate all leftovers.

Desserts

Rhubarb Surprise Cake

SERVINGS 12 • PREP TIME 10 minutes • COOK TIME 1 hour

- 5 cups chopped rhubarb
- 1 cup sugar
- 3 oz. pkg. strawberry gelatin
- 3 cups mini marshmallows
- 1 box white cake mix
- Cool Whip (optional)

1. Preheat oven to 375° F. Spray a 9" x 13" baking dish with cooking spray. Place rhubarb in baking dish.
2. Combine sugar and gelatin. Sprinkle mixture over rhubarb. Top with marshmallows.
3. Mix cake as directed on package and pour over mixture in cake pan.
4. Bake 60 minutes. Top with Cool Whip, if desired.

Rhubarb Upside Down Cake

SERVINGS 8 • PREP TIME 15 minutes • COOK TIME 45 minutes

- 3 cups rhubarb, chopped
- 1½ cups mini marshmallows
- 1 sm. box strawberry gelatin
- ½ cup granulated sugar
- 1 box yellow cake mix
- ½ cup brown sugar

1. Preheat oven to 350° F. Place rhubarb into buttered cake pan. Sprinkle with marshmallows.
2. Combine gelatin and sugar in small mixing bowl and sprinkle over marshmallows.
3. Prepare cake mix according to package. Pour over fruit mixture in pan.
4. Sprinkle brown sugar over the top. Bake for 45 minutes. Serve warm with whipped cream or ice cream.

Desserts

Snowball Cake

SERVINGS 12 • PREP TIME 30 minutes • COOK TIME 1 hour

- 1 box devil's food cake mix
- 1 8 oz. pkg. cream cheese, softened
- 1 egg
- 2 Tbs. sugar

Frosting:
- 1 sm. pkg. vanilla instant pudding
- 1 cup milk
- 8 oz. Cool Whip
- 1 cup coconut flakes
- 2 cups powdered sugar

1 Prepare cake as directed on package. Pour into oven-safe bowl and set aside.

2 In separate bowl, combine cream cheese, egg, and sugar until well blended. Pour into center of cake batter, keeping it in the middle.

3 Bake at 350° F. for 1 hour or until toothpick stuck into center comes out clean.

4 Cool in bowl 10 minutes.

5 Loosen cake from sides of bowl and invert onto wire rack. Let cool completely. (Can be placed in freezer for an hour.)

6 Meanwhile, beat powdered sugar, pudding and milk in med. bowl for two minutes until well blended. Put in refrigerator until ready to use.

7 When cake has cooled, place on serving platter. Frost, then sprinkle with coconut. Keep refrigerated.

Sweet Potato Cake

SERVINGS 12 • PREP TIME 15 minutes • COOK TIME 45 minutes

- 1 cup vegetable oil
- 2 cups sugar
- 4 eggs
- 1½ cups finely shredded sweet potato
- ¼ cup hot water
- 1 tsp. vanilla
- 3½ cups self-rising flour
- 1 tsp. ground cinnamon
- 1 cup sliced almonds

Frosting:
- ½ cup butter
- 1 cup packed brown sugar
- 1 cup evaporated milk
- 3 egg yolks, beaten
- 1½ cups coconut flakes
- 1 tsp. vanilla

1. Preheat oven to 350° F. In mixing bowl, beat oil and sugar. Add eggs in one at a time, beating well after each addition.

2. Add sweet potato, water, and vanilla, mixing well.

3. Combine flour and cinnamon and add to batter. Stir in almonds.

4. Pour into greased 9" x 13" pan. Bake for 40 t0 45 minutes, or until toothpick comes out clean from center.

5. Prepare frosting: Melt butter in saucepan. Whisk in sugar, milk, and egg yolks until smooth.

6. Bring to a boil over med. heat. Boil gently for 2 minutes. Remove from heat

7. Stir in coconut flakes, almonds, and vanilla. Spread over warm cake. Cool on wire rack.

Desserts

Triple Chocolate Triple Layer Cake

SERVINGS 12 • PREP TIME 25 minutes • COOK TIME 15 minutes

- 1 box Betty Crocker Triple Chocolate with Chocolate Chips cake mix
- ⅔ cup unsweetened Ghirardelli cocoa powder
- ½ cup butter
- 1 tsp. vanilla
- 6 cups powdered sugar
- ½ cup milk (approximately)

1. Prepare cake as directed on box. Spray three 8-inch round cake pans with cooking spray and lightly dust with flour.

2. Pour ⅓ of batter into each pan. Bake at 350° F. for 12 to 15 minutes. Cake will bounce back in the middle when done, or poke with toothpick in the center; when toothpick comes out clean, cake is done.

3. Cool 15 minutes. Place in freezer in cake pans. Let freeze for 4 hours or overnight. (Can make ahead and place in freezer bags until ready to use.)

4. Prepare frosting: Mix cocoa powder, butter, and vanilla until creamy. Slowly add powdered sugar, about a cup at a time.

5. Drizzle in milk after each addition to make thick consistency. Frosting should be thick but spreadable. If it is too thin, add more powdered sugar. If too thick, add a few drops of milk.

7-Minute Frosting

FROSTS 2 layer cakes • PREP TIME 10 minutes • COOK TIME 0 minutes

- 1¾ cups granulated sugar
- ½ cup cold water
- 1 Tbs. light corn syrup
- 2 egg whites
- ⅛ tsp. salt
- 1 tsp. vanilla

1 In top of double boiler, combine all ingredients except vanilla. Place over rapidly boiling water; the top pan should not touch the water.

2 Beat with hand mixer at highest speed until mixture stands in peaks, about 7 minutes. Do not overcook.

3 Remove from heat and add vanilla. Continue beating until frosting holds deep swirls, about 2 minutes.

*Will be more than enough for a 2 layer cake.

Butter Cream Frosting

FROSTS 2 layer cakes • PREP TIME 10 minutes • COOK TIME 0 minutes

- ⅔ cup butter, softened
- 4 cups powdered sugar
- 1 tsp. vanilla
- 2 to 4 Tbs. milk

1 In lg. bowl, beat butter until smooth. Slowly add powdered sugar, beating well. Beat in vanilla.

2 Add milk until frosting is the consistency you want for the cake you are frosting.

Desserts

Chocolate Frosting

FROSTS 2 layer cakes • PREP TIME 10 minutes • COOK TIME 0 minutes

- ¼ cup Crisco
- ½ cup unsweetened cocoa powder
- ¼ tsp. salt
- ⅓ cup milk
- 2 Tbs. vanilla
- 3½ cups powdered sugar

1 In med. saucepan, melt the Crisco over low heat. Remove from heat and add cocoa and salt.

2 Stir in milk and vanilla. Put sugar in a bowl and add chocolate mixture. Mix at med. speed until smooth and creamy.

3 Add 1 Tbs. more milk if necessary.

Chocolate Glaze

FROSTS 1 cake • PREP TIME 10 minutes • COOK TIME 0 minutes

- 2 cups powdered sugar
- 2 Tbs. butter, softened
- 2 oz. unsweetened chocolate, melted
- 1 tsp. vanilla or almond extract
- 3 to 4 Tbs. milk

1 In med. bowl, combine all ingredients, adding enough milk for desired glaze consistency.

2 Drizzle over Bundt cake.

Mixing bowls, cutting boards and cookie sheets will not move if a damp towel is placed under them.

Desserts

Cream Cheese Frosting

FROSTS 2 layer cakes • PREP TIME 10 minutes • COOK TIME 0 minutes

- 3 cups powdered sugar
- 1 8 oz. pkg. cream cheese
- 2 Tbs. butter, melted
- 1 tsp. vanilla

1 Combine all ingredients in bowl until fluffy and smooth.

Coconut Pecan Frosting

FROSTS 2 layer cakes • PREP TIME 10 minutes • COOK TIME 0 minutes

- 1 cup sugar
- 1 cup evaporated milk
- ½ cup butter
- 3 eggs, beaten
- 1½ cups coconut flakes
- 1 cup chopped pecans
- 1 tsp. vanilla

1 In med. saucepan, combine sugar, milk, butter, and eggs.

2 Cook over med. heat until mixture starts to bubble, stirring constantly.

3 Stir in rest of the ingredients. Cool mixture to the desired consistency.

Desserts

Creamy Chocolate Frosting

MAKES 6 cups frosting • PREP TIME 10 minutes
COOK TIME 0 minutes

- ⅔ cup unsweetened Ghirardelli cocoa powder
- ½ cup butter
- 1 tsp. vanilla
- 6 cups powdered sugar
- ½ cup milk (approximately)

1. Mix chocolate powder, butter, and vanilla until creamy.

2. Slowly add powdered sugar, about a cup at a time.

3. Drizzle in milk after each addition to make thick consistency. Frosting should be thick, but spreadable. If it is too thin, add in more powdered sugar. If too thick, add a few drops of milk.

Light, Creamy Frosting

FROSTS 2 layer cakes or 9" x 13" cake • PREP TIME 10 minutes
COOK TIME 0 minutes

- 1 pkg. any flavor instant pudding
- ¾ cup cold milk
- ¼ cup powdered sugar
- 8 oz. whipped topping

1. With electric mixer, beat pudding, milk, and powdered sugar for about 1 minute.

2. Fold in whipped topping.

3. Leftover frosting can be refrigerated.

Desserts

Fluffy-As-a-Cloud Frosting

**FROSTS 2 layer cakes or 9" x 13" cake • PREP TIME 5 minutes
COOK TIME 20 minutes**

- 2¼ cups granulated sugar
- 1 cup water
- 2 Tbs. light corn syrup
- ⅛ tsp. salt
- 3 extra lg. egg whites
- 1 tsp. vanilla

1. In med. saucepan, combine sugar, water, corn syrup, and salt. Over low heat, stir until sugar dissolves.

2. Attach a candy thermometer to side of pan and turn heat up to med. high. Bring to boil and cook until mixture reaches 240° F. Do not stir.

3. Meanwhile, put egg whites in lg. mixing bowl, and beat on high with hand mixer until stiff peaks form. When syrup mixture reaches 240° F, slowly trickle hot syrup into beaten egg whites.

4. Add vanilla and keep beating on high until frosting is thick enough to hold stiff peaks.

No-Weep Meringue

FROSTS 1 pie • PREP TIME 25 minutes • COOK TIME 15 minutes

- ½ cup cold water
- 1 Tbs. cornstarch
- 3 Tbs. sugar
- 3 egg whites

1. Combine water, cornstarch, and sugar in med. saucepan. Cook until thick. Cool.

2. In mixing bowl, beat egg whites until light peaks form. Add to cooled mixture and beat until blended.

3. Pour over pie and brown in oven until peaks are golden.

Index

APPETIZERS & SAUCES
Baked Hot Wings, 17
Cheese Ball, 17
Cocktail Sauce, 18
Creamy Onion Dip (light), 18
Deviled Eggs, 19
French Onion Dip, 19
Fruit Dip, 20
Fruit Kabobs, 20
Garlic and Chile Sauce, 21
Guacamole Dip, 22
Ham Mustard Glaze, 22
Meat & Veggie Egg Rolls, 23
Simple Sweet & Sour Sauce, 23
Parmesan Chicken Appetizer, 24
Pinecone Log, 24
Taco Dip, 25
Tartar Sauce, 25
Traditional Meatballs, 26
White Chocolate Party Mix, 27

BREADS & BREAKFASTS
Apple Banana Bread, 31
Apricot Cranberry Bread, 32
Banana Bread, 31
Blueberry Buckle, 33
Breakfast Burritos, 33
Caramel Breakfast Rolls, 34
Cheesy Garlic Biscuits, 34
Chocolate and Biscuits, 35
Chocolate Sour Cream
   Coffee Cake, 36
Cinnamon Rolls, 37
Coffee Cake, 38
Corn Bread, 35
Cranberry Nut Muffins, 41
Crescent Rolls, 39
Dinner Rolls, 40
Easy Drop Danish, 41
French Breakfast Muffins, 42
Gingerbread, 43
Lemon Bread, 37
Monkey Bread, 45
Pancakes & Waffles, 44
Pumpkin Bread, 45
Rhubarb-Pecan Muffins, 46
Sausage Quiche, 46
Streusel Topping, 38
Zucchini Bread, 47

BEVERAGES
Banana-Orange Honey Shake, 51
Cranberry Apple Cider, 51
Hot Apple Cider, 52
Hot Chocolate Mix, 52
Hot Fruit Drink, 53
Orange Julius, 53
Party Punch, 54
Spice Tea Mix, 54

SALADS & DRESSINGS
Broccoli Salad, 57
Chicken Salad on Croissants, 57
Creamy Cranberry Salad, 58
Crunchy Tuna Salad, 59
Cucumber Salad, 59
Egg Salad, 60
Fresh Asparagus Salad, 60
Fruit Salad, 61
Italian Pasta Salad, 62
Jell-O Salad, 62
Lemony Chicken Salad, 63
Macaroni Salad, 63
Oriental Chicken Salad, 64
Pear & Walnut Spring Mix Salad, 64
Potato Salad, 65

Summer Fruit Salad, 66
Summer Special Salad, 67
Tossed Salad with Walnuts & Cranberries, 68
Turkey Salad, 68
Creamy Celery Seed Dressing, 58
Garlic Lemon Buttermilk Dressing, 61
Red Wine Vinaigrette Dressing, 66
Thousand Island Dressing, 67

SOUPS & STEWS
Beef Stew, 71
Chicken & Vegetable Soup, 71
Chicken Tortilla Soup, 72
Chili, 73
Corn Chowder Soup, 72
Cream of Broccoli Soup, 73
Cream of Potato Soup, 74
Crock of Steak, 75
Hamburger or Chicken Soup, 74

MAIN DISHES
Baked Chicken, 79
Baked Chicken Swiss, 79
Beef & Bean Green Chile Burritos, 80
Cashew Chicken Stir Fry, 81
Chicken Bake with Wild Rice, 80
Chicken Alfredo, 82
Chicken and Biscuit Casserole, 83
Chicken Enchiladas, 84
Chicken Kiev, 85
Chicken Pot Pie, 86
Chicken Stir Fry, 88
Chicken Taco Casserole, 89
Chicken with Pineapple, 87
Cornish Game Hens with Garlic & Rosemary, 90
Cube Steaks with White Gravy, 91
Deluxe Chicken Enchiladas, 92
Italian Sausage and Vegetable Linguini, 91
Lemon Teriyaki Glazed Chicken, 83
Meatloaf, 89
Non-Fried Fish & Chips with Slaw, 93
Parmesan Chicken, 94
Parmesan Pepper Steak, 94
Pork Chop Casserole, 95
Pork Chops with Cranberry Mustard Sauce, 96
Pot Roast, 97
Pork Roast or Chops with Ginger Sauce, 95
Red Chile Enchiladas, 98
Rice & Beef Hot Dish, 98
Roasted Lemon Herb Chicken, 99
Salisbury Steak, 100
Sausage & Peppers with Bow Tie Pasta, 99
Savory Pepper Steak, 101
Sloppy Joes, 101
Spaghetti with Meat Sauce, 102
Succulent Baked Chicken, 103
Teriyaki Chicken, 103
Teriyaki Chicken Kabobs, 104
Tuna & Biscuits with White Gravy, 104

SIDE DISHES
Baby Glazed Carrots, 107
Baked Asparagus with Parmesan, 107
Baked Beans, 108
Baked Stuffed Zucchini, 108
Baked Sweet Potatoes, 109
Black Beans, 109
Broccoli Casserole, 110
Candied Yams, 110
Corn Casserole, 111
Country Baked Beans, 111

Crunchy Potato Bake, 112
Easy Potato Casserole, 112
Green Bean Casserole, 113
Green Bean Melody, 113
Homemade French Fries, 114
Mashed Sweet Potatoes, 114
Mexican Coleslaw, 115
Old Fashioned Scalloped Potatoes, 115
Oven Baked Fried Potatoes, 116
Oven Roasted Potatoes, 116
Party Potatoes, 117
Red Beans & Rice, 118
Red Potatoes Baked or Grilled, 117
Spanish Rice, 118
Spinach Soufflé, 119
Twice Baked Potatoes, 120
Wagon Wheel Pasta with Salsa-Marinated Beans, 121

DESSERTS
Cookies
Almond Glazed Sugar Cookies, 125
Butterscotch Chocolate-Chip Cookies, 134
Cake Mix Cookies, 134
Chocolate-Chip Cookies, 126
Chocolate Coconut Balls, 126
Coconut Islands Cookies, 127
Cowboy Cookies, 128
Gluten Free Peanut Butter Cookies, 128
Grandma's Favorite Sugar Cookies, 129
Lazy Boy Sugar Cookies, 129
Oatmeal Chocolate-Chip Cookies, 130
Oreo Truffles, 130
Peanut Blossoms, 131
Peanut Butter Cookies, 131
Pumpkin Orange Cookies, 132
Rolled Sugar Cookies, 133
Snicker Doodles, 127

Cakes
Apple Cake, 135
Berry Chocolate Cream Cake, 136
Black Forest Cake, 137
Carrot Cake, 138
Cherry Cheesecake, 139
Chocolate Cake with Raspberry Sauce, 139
Country Apple Cake with Caramel Sauce, 140
Drummer Boy Cake, 141
Dump Cake, 142
Low-Calorie, Low-Fat Cake, 142
Mayonnaise Cake, 143
Mocha Pudding Cake, 143
Orange Kiss-Me Cake, 144
Oreo Cheesecake, 144
Pumpkin Spice Cake, 145
Red Velvet Cupcakes, 146
Red Velvet Pound Cake, 147
Rhubarb Cake, 147
Rhubarb Surprise Cake, 148
Rhubarb Upside Down Cake, 148
Snowball Cake, 149
Sweet Potato Cake, 150
Triple Chocolate Triple Layer Cake, 151

Frostings
7 Minute Frosting, 152
Butter Cream Frosting, 152
Chocolate Frosting, 153
Chocolate Glaze, 153
Coconut Pecan Frosting, 154
Cream Cheese Frosting, 154
Creamy Chocolate Frosting, 155
Fluffy-As-a-Cloud Frosting, 156
Light, Creamy Frosting, 155
No-Weep Meringue, 156

To request Janet for a speaking event or for catering a special event, you may contact her at familydinner@live.com.

To order additional copies of this cookbook, go to www.givingtons.com.